Mindfulness 360

A Holistic Path to Clarity, Balance & Peace

CALM
Technique
— Heal-Thy —

Narin Kalra (Vivekarthi)

PG PUBLICATION

Delhi- 110089 (India)

Edition : 2026
ISBN : 978-93-6210-383-3

Price : 495/-

Mindfulness 360
A Holistic Path to Clarity, Balance & Peace
Narin Kalra (Vivekarthi)
Mail id : narinkalra17@gmail.com

Cover Page & Book Layout
Pooja Kanojiya

Published by
PRAKHAR GOONJ PUBLICATIONS
Office : A-11/90, Sector-18 Rohini, Delhi-110089
Reg. Office : H-3/2 Sector-18 Rohini, Delhi-110089
Email : prakhargoonj@gmail.com
info@prakhargoonjpublications.com
Ph. : 7982710571, 7838505899, 011-42635077
Web : prakhargoonjpublications.com

Dedicated to

All Aspirants on the path of Awareness, Compassion and Inner growth.

Acknowledgement

I would like to acknowledge the profound influence of the teachings and writings of Jon Kabat-Zinn, Kristin Neff, and Tara Brach. Their work on mindfulness, compassion, and inner awareness has deeply inspired my reflections and has helped shape the perspectives shared in this book.

Author's Note

This book emerged from a simple but profound curiosity: how can we live with greater awareness, gratitude, and compassion in the midst of everyday life?

Many of the reflections in these pages grew out of my personal practice of mindfulness and self-inquiry. Over time, I began to notice how the mind often moves quickly from one thought to another, rarely pausing long enough to understand itself. Mindfulness, for me, became a gentle invitation to slow down, to observe the flow of experience moment by moment, and to discover the quiet wisdom that already resides within.

The ideas explored here have been inspired in part by the teachings from Buddhism and by the writings and research of Jon Kabat-Zinn, Kristin Neff, and Tara Brach. Their work on mindfulness and compassion has helped bring these practices into contemporary life.

Their insights have been deeply influential in shaping my understanding and approach to these reflections.

This book does not claim to offer definitive answers. Rather, it is an invitation to pause, to reflect, and to explore the inner landscape of our own experience, with curiosity and kindness.

If these reflections encourage even a brief moment of awareness or gratitude in the reader's life, then the purpose of this work will have been fulfilled.

Foreword

This book offers something both rare and necessary- original thinking expressed in a practical, usable way.

It's ideas are not abstract theories meant to impress; they are living concepts meant to be practiced. Each page carries reflections that are thoughtful yet grounded, innovative yet deeply human. The strength of this work lies in its ability to translate insight into application. Complex emotional and relational dynamics are presented with clarity, making them accessible without losing depth.

What makes this book distinctive is simplicity of application and the depth of its implications. The principles shared here are not distant ideals; they are immediately usable in daily life- in conversations, in conflict, in self-reflection, and in healing. The reader is not overwhelmed with instruction but gently guided toward awareness and practice.

Prof. (Dr.) Rekha Sapra
Professor,
Dept. Of Human Development & Family Empowerment
University Of Delhi
India

Foreword

In today's fast-moving and often stressful world, finding clarity and balance within ourselves has become more important than ever. Mindfulness 360: A Holistic Path to Clarity, Balance & Peace by Narin Kalra (Vivekarthi) is a thoughtful and practical guide in this direction.

This book encourages us to slow down, observe our thoughts, and reconnect with ourselves. It is based on the ideas of mindfulness, self-awareness, and compassion, but it presents them in a very simple and easy-to-understand way.

One of the strengths of this book is that it connects ideas with real life. It does not remain limited to theory but shows how mindfulness can be applied in everyday situations like stress, decision-making, and relationships. The practices shared in the book, such as CALM, RAIN, and PEACE, are simple tools that anyone can use in daily life.

The author writes with honesty and clarity, making the reader feel guided rather than instructed. The book helps us become more aware of our thoughts and emotions, and gradually move from reacting automatically to responding more calmly and thoughtfully.

As publishers, we are happy to present a book that adds real value to readers' lives. It has the potential to support people in understanding themselves better and finding a sense of inner balance.

I believe this book will connect with a wide range of readers. Its message is simple, practical, and relevant to everyday life.

I wish the author the very best and hope that this book proves helpful to many people on their journey toward clarity and peace.

Neelu Sinha
Founder & Editor-in-Chief
Prakhar Goonj Publications

Contents

SECTION
I

Introduction

Mindfulness- A first step towards self-reflection

There are moments in life when we feel shattered and broken. In those moments of vulnerability, it seems as if we are sinking, feeling emotionally drowned in an ocean of stress, anxiety, and depression.

A sense of helplessness arises and we feel emotionally overwhelmed and burnt out.

Devastation may result from work overload and excessive responsibilities; it may also stem from a sense of inadequacy. At times, relationships may present challenges. We might also come across financial crisis. Possibly, there may be a traumatic experience that may shake us from within.

Gradually, all these experiences accumulate. Their impact is multi-layered and have an aggregative effect on our Mental and Physical wellness.

The challenges thrown by life results in insomnia, elevated stress, and a feeling of insecurity. We might end up with a feeling of worthlessness and guilt.

The minute we identify those moments of vulnerability, we not only become aware of these anomalies, but also become a witness to our sufferings, pain, and agony that we are going through at times.

Acknowledging our weaknesses is the first small step toward addressing them. It builds resilience, strengthens our ability to handle challenges, and encourages the self-reflection needed to overcome weaknesses.

Seeking support becomes essential for growth and

improvement. We can aid ourselves by seeking guidance from Practitioners or Therapists.

Mindfulness is an opening to self-awareness, a first step towards self-reflection. Regularly taking time to reflect on our thoughts can help identify any negative thought patterns, and we may consciously and gradually start shifting towards a more positive outlook.

Do not consider Mindfulness as a substitute for medication or therapy, specifically in cases where medication is part of necessary treatment plans. Mindfulness should be considered as a complementary approach, more as a supplement, and not a replacement for any ongoing treatment.

CHAPTER 1
The Riches of Life

Everything in this universe is in constant motion, governed by natural laws.

Always on the move, no matter what happens, acting in accordance with Laws set by Nature.

We, as part of this Universe are bound to follow the same set of rules, and so is our personal universe is invariably in motion.

Our mind always remains restless, like a hamster running, exploring, and climbing around inside its little hamster cage.

This mind is not just running around, but has immense power of creativity, power of imagination and power to visualize, and on top of that, the mind is versatile. Mind's versatility allows us to create, imagine, learn, experience, and feel.

Due to its agility, the mind gets the ability to connect with others, to see and sense their emotions and form common bond with others through empathy and understanding.

Sometimes our mind behaves like a stubborn child, and other times it becomes our counsellor.

Mind is a whole spectrum of vivid characteristics, on occasion the mind is full of vibrancy and vitality, and other moments may become sluggish and passive.

To better understand the mind, we may use an analogy in modern terms. Imagine the mind as a virtual cloud- a vast, dynamic space that stores and processes endless streams of data.

As an infinite flow of information and impressions flows in through our senses, our mind is constantly processing, gathering, storing and retrieving information.

Every sight, sound, smell, touch, or taste; every experience and memory. Every imagination and dream- all of these pass through the mind.

Even the simple sensation of touching wet clay, the warmth of a welcome, or an annoying rude tone- each moment leaves an imprint that is recorded and stored, often without our conscious awareness. A succession of instances creates a continuous mental and emotional stream. The events arise and pass away, one after another.

As we move through life, we carry these impressions within us.

The practice of Mindfulness is remembering to pay attention to our experiences, every moment, moment by moment.

When we engage with awareness, we begin to uncover the depth of these experiences- illuminating hidden insights and awakening the wisdom that already resides within.

When the mind denies accepting an experience, the body volunteers to store that experience.

Resulting in a mental experience being suppressed and relocated to the body, resulting in an impact on mental, emotional, and physical health.

We are always surrounded by unpredictability and surprises. This is an ever-changing Universe, never stopping, never resting. The only thing that does not change is 'the Change'. Everything is bound to change except 'the Change' itself.

Mind is a dynamic and scalable field of awareness, constantly adapting to new experiences.

Every one of us has the capability to harness the stream of events passing through the mind and achieve the Great Riches of Life.

1. **The Riches of Health**

First and foremost, the true Riches of life inhabit in our Health. Good health is often overlooked as a form of wealth, yet it is the very foundation of our existence. It is that supports every aspect of our being and provides the energy and strength to chase our passions.

Health is a priceless gift that, once compromised, becomes hard to recover and sometimes impossible to replace. Health is the basis of true wealth, and the pillar of life. When we talk of health, that includes holistic health, not just physical health, but mental and emotional health as well.

2. **The Riches of Emotional Stability**

Emotional stability is another essential dimension of Riches. It is the inner strength that nurtures growth, enables us to face challenges with courage and reveals the strength and resilience within us.

Emotional stability is a basic element in building resilience, understanding, and self-confidence within us. It allows us to remain balanced amidst uncertainty and crisis.

3. **The Riches of a Calm Mind**

A calm mind cannot be compared to any material possession. A calm mind surpasses any materialistic comparison and can be harder to achieve, than said.

Peace of mind is the ultimate form of Riches. It's the inner calm that brings contentment, allowing us to sleep soundly and greet each day with an open heart.

4. The Riches of Wisdom

Wisdom is a significant part of our existence. It enables us to perceive the meaning of life with clarity and to gain perspective through our experiences. Wisdom grows through a sincere desire to learn from our own experiences and the experiences we go through during interactions with others. Everything adds up.

This is a lifelong process that is shaped by numerous factors like openness to learning, retention of meaningful experiences and the application of those experiences.

Being True to Yourself- There is a quiet beauty in authenticity- a raw grace that arises from being genuine. Being true to yourself is the most essential part of our existence.

I began reflecting on what it really means to be True to oneself.

By and large, it is about authenticity, being true to yourself, sincere with your own self. It is about living in harmony with who you are and honouring your values, your emotions, and the natural way you move through life.

When our actions and choices are in alignment with our inner truth, we experience a sense of Peace of mind and a feeling of integrity.

Being authentic to yourself does not require validation or praise from others and it's not about being perfect, but it is living in sync with what you think is reasonable and what you stand for.

To be true to yourself means living with awareness and noticing the drifts that carry you away from your real self, and a gentle return, a shift from 'performing actor' to a 'Real Being'.

And in that 'Real Being', lies the Riches of freedom and Integrity.

Mindfulness is the key to unlocking these great inner Riches. It turns ordinary moments into deep, meaningful lessons, which we apply in real life. (Kabat-Zinn, Full Catastrophe Living Using the Wisdom of Your Body and Mind to Face Stress, Pain and Illness, 2013)

We invite you to begin a journey with us to discover ways of a holistic lifestyle with reduced stress. It all comes with practice, self-reflection, and awareness of the present moment. Mindfulness practice is not about silencing the mind, or trying to suppress the thoughts, rather, it suggests cultivating our minds with gentle awareness.

CHAPTER 2
Life: A Collage of Moments

Life, in itself, is a complete package of experiences.

It can be viewed as an arena where we encounter fresh challenges, interact with diverse people, face real-life problems, deal with anger, and, at times, experience aggression.

At the same time, life can also be viewed as a continuous workshop that provides opportunities to grow, where we develop our skills and learn to improve our relationships with others. We learn to manage stress more effectively and engage with people with greater awareness and a thoughtful presence. Life sometimes offers action-oriented adventures, adventures that are filled with puzzles and surprises.

Whatsoever we see life as a bouquet of moments, memories, and challenges.

Whether at work, while travelling or shopping, we all need to make choices and are often compelled to take decisions or make selections. Even at home, we have to decide what to cook or not, or to skip the meal, or shall I just order something online, or even go out for a nice dinner.

While intending to relax, we come across so many choices. Choosing a streaming service, browsing through countless shows, and finally picking something to watch, indeed, it is not an easy task to make decision.

Making work related decisions may not always be easy, it requires a diverse skill set, an awareness of workplace ethics and an understanding of workplace culture and conditions.

Every situation is unique by itself and demands a unique response and a well-reasoned decision.

Our responses play a crucial role in shaping our ongoing emotional experiences and determining who we are. Our reactions shape our reality.

Sometimes our responses are driven by anger or stress, potentially the outcomes may get aggravated and likely add to fear, anger, or stress.

On the other hand, when we are responding calmly to a situation with control over our emotions that leads to a certain level of positive experience.

This is where mindfulness comes into play, by bringing our attention to the present moment, mindfulness allows us to see our thoughts and emotions with elevated awareness.

During those moments of awareness we start acknowledging reality, noticing the occurrences with a clearer vision. Instead of criticizing ourselves or others, we get inclined towards a neutral attitude, looking at things as they are, with no commentary or judgments. We gradually turn more realistic. Gradually, we start noticing change in ourselves, the transformation makes us more composed, in control, and unshaken. We begin to be responsive instead of reactive. There are no more spontaneous reactions.

Our reactions create a mental energy that significantly influences the way we look at the world around us and how we perceive the universe.

Resource:

Mindfulness Session 1:
Mindfulness with Busy Life Style

Life can be viewed as a continuous workshop where we learn and refine our mindfulness skills and explore and develop new dimensions of mindfulness along the way.

Every day, we encounter fresh challenges, interact with diverse individuals, and face real-life situations. Whether at the workplace, while travelling, while shopping or even at home. Every situation demands a decision and a response.

Our responses play a pivotal role in shaping our ongoing emotional experiences.

If we respond to a situation with fear, anger, or stress that can significantly influence our perception of the world.

Conversely, when we respond with mindfulness along with emotional regulation, it can lead to more positive and balanced experiences.

Mindfulness, a practice of being fully aware and present in the moment, aids to make wiser choices and responding more effectively.

Through conscious practice of mindfulness, we evolve into a better version of ourselves, becoming more adaptive, handling stress and nurturing our relationships.

The more intentionally we apply mindfulness, the better we get prepared to make informed decisions and choose our responses wisely.

CHAPTER 3
Live in the Moment with Yourself

The interesting fact about mindfulness is that we consciously choose to live in the present moment with full awareness. Living in the moment allows us to observe and differentiate various mental activities, giving us a clearer and more balanced perspective.

Just as physicists use differential calculus to determine the path of a projectile by analyzing variables such as speed, acceleration, and gravity to describe its trajectory, even though for a Spacecraft hundreds of thousands of miles away. Most importantly all these variants are functions of Time. These values are continuously changing from moment to moment.

Mindfulness works in a similar way. It helps us to observe and differentiate the trajectory of thoughts, allowing us to distinguish between thoughts and feelings with greater clarity. It cultivates a deeper understanding of what we are feeling, what we are thinking and what we are doing.

This transforms the habit of auto-reaction into a conscious knower's response.

One of the most meaningful transformations is that we start to develop an improvised ability to navigate through rough times with greater clarity and peace.

Mindful practice is an everyday living practice, a way of living in each moment with full awareness. Awareness is the key ingredient of mindfulness; it transforms practice into a way of life.

Mindfulness is not about stopping our work or withdrawing from responsibilities, rather, it is about performing all our daily activities with full awareness, intentionally and purposefully bringing our attention to every aspect of that moment.

We may start with our breath, as it is the most obvious aspect of our lives available to us 24 hours a day, constantly available every moment. Most of the time the breath goes unnoticed due to its subtle movement and quiet presence.

Let us perform one breathing cycle with awareness. Observe this gentle movement of air as we breathe in and out.

As you breathe in, notice how the abdomen gently expands during inhalation. Recognize that you are breathing in and allow your awareness to move with the flow of air travelling inward. Observe a brief, natural pause before you begin to breathe out.

As you start to exhale, let your awareness follow the outgoing air, recognize that you are breathing out, be aware of the soft movement of the abdomen while exhaling. Simply notice the flow of air, witness the natural rhythm of the breath without trying to control or manipulate it.

These are among the most visible movements of the body, yet they are rarely observed. As we begin observing these movements, we awaken our awareness for the Present Moment.

Present Moment Awareness is a wholesome recollection of what is unfolding right now in this moment, knowing our experiences and noticing the subtle physical feelings in that moment.

As we begin practicing mindfulness, we often notice that the mind seems to becomes more active. Many thoughts start rushing into the mind. The mind is engaged in planning and creating stories. It begins to move forward into the future or it bounces back into loops of past memories.

It keeps travelling, anticipating what is to come or replaying what has already happened.

The present moment, however, is subtle and brief. It does not offer much space for the mind to roam around. The mind starts becoming restless, as if it feels confined in a narrow space of the present moment

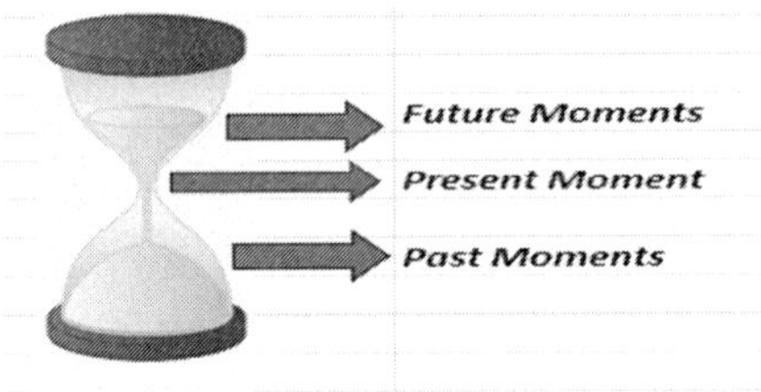

Let us loosen the reins of the mind. Let it fly. Allow thoughts to flow freely, like a river streaming. And let yourself be an observer, not an evaluator. Watch your mind as a beginner, with beginner's curiosity, see everything as you are seeing for the first time.

Gradually, the thoughts will begin to slow down, and this is the moment when you bring your attention to the awareness of thoughts.

When you are breathing, know that you are breathing. When you are hearing, simply hear.

We listen attentively. When we see, we see mindfully. When we touch, we touch mindfully, with care and presence. In this way, we listen to our own thoughts with full awareness.

Experienced practitioners often say mindfulness feels like watching a slideshow of random scenes, passing one right after another. At times it is like watching a video game rather than playing it- there is no pressure, no urgency

Mindfulness is not a passive detachment from the world, rather, it is full participation in life, but without worrying about winning or losing. It is engagement without pressure, involvement without fear.

The goal, then, is not to silence the mind but to stand-in a state of mindful observation, where thoughts arise and pass without resistance, no judgments, but with full awareness. Like waves rising and falling on the surface of the ocean, each thought has a beginning, middle, and an end. By developing a gentle awareness, we can acknowledge the movement of the mind without feeling compelled to control it.

The journey becomes less about controlling the uncontrollable and more about letting go and accepting.

I had heard a lot about mindfulness, and the idea interested me. I first tried to set aside some time to sit quietly to practice mindfulness and observe my mind.

One evening, I found a comfortable spot, closed my eyes, and set a timer for five minutes.

Five minutes didn't sound like much- until I started. Within the next three minutes, I checked my stopwatch twice, it felt if the time had slowed down.

I noticed just how restless my mind was. Thoughts started coming rapidly.

Did I take my morning medication?

Was the door locked from inside?

What am I cooking for tonight?

I realized how frequently my mind was jumping from one thought to the next.

There were moments when I began to feel anxious.

Why can't I focus? Why am I so restless? Why is it so hard for me to concentrate?

But then, something interesting happened. Instead of

trying to control or quiet my thoughts, I just watched. But I didn't push them away. I just let them flow. I felt like an outsider peeking into this inner world, never lasting too long on any one thing.

Over time, these short sessions taught me that my mind had its own pace, its own way of moving from thought to thought. By stepping back as an observer, I discovered that I didn't have to struggle with my mind to find peace. I found a certain calm in simply being present in the moment, knowing it would keep flowing, moment by moment.

When we practice mindfulness, we may observe our mind acting like a curious child, jumping from one thought to the next, dwelling on past mistakes, or worrying about future challenges. But with gentle observation, we can learn to watch these thoughts without becoming entangled in them.

Remember that each moment is filled with events, and there has never been a moment in the universe without something happening.

By becoming aware of each passing moment, we can let go of our tendency to be critical or judgmental and simply feel what we're feeling.

Mindfulness is the protector of the mind and the proctor of awareness. As a protector, it shields the mind from straying away.

As a proctor, it supervises our actions, making sure they remain steady, clear, and unbiased.

It ensures the mind does not drift and maintains a balance between faith and wisdom.

While walking through a shopping mall, my eyes suddenly fixed on an exquisite watch displayed in a showroom. The timepiece was so elegant and rustic, its presence so alluring that my mind began to drag me toward it. I imagined how perfect it would look on my wrist. I wanted that expensive timepiece badly.

But then, the mind acted like a proctor, mindfulness stepped in and asked: "Why do you need this watch right now?"

I already own a watch, and rarely do I even wear one. A watch simply tells the correct time.

Mindfulness caught the thought of buying. My heart was pounding fast, pulled by the desire to own that timepiece. Yet I noticed the craving, and in that moment, awareness reminded me: even in the presence of longing, I do not have to be carried away.

I walked on, leaving the watch behind, but carrying with me something far more valuable- freedom.

This is the art of awareness- experiencing each passing moment as it is.

Resource:

Mindfulness Session 2:
Living in Present Moment

(Kabat-Zinn, Guided Mindfulness Meditation, 2014)

Welcome to this new session of mindfulness practice.

The present moment is the only true time available to us, and it holds immense value for our well-being and self-care.

Let's embrace these precious moments and dedicate them to nurturing ourselves.

Practicing mindfulness can significantly enhance the quality of our lives as it embraces a holistic approach to well-being.

Let's ground ourselves in this present moment.

Find a comfortable posture with an upright back and relaxed shoulders. Gently close your eyes and breathe naturally.

Direct your attention to the breath.

Focus on the area where you perceive the breath most distinctly, whether it's at the tip of your nose, the nostrils, the chest, or the abdomen.

Simply stay with the breath for a while. Allow your breath to flow normally, without any effort or manipulation. Keep breathing.

Let's continue our practice, even during these periods of silence.

(30 sec silence)

Let the chime of this bell serve as a gentle reminder

to redirect your focus back to your breath whenever your mind starts wandering.

Stay with your breath with full awareness in this moment.

And in this moment,

And in this moment.

Moment-by-moment.

Embrace the power of the present moment, cultivating a deep sense of awareness as you consciously connect with your breath.

Whenever you notice your mind has wandered away from the breath, gently redirect your attention back to it.

Practice mindfulness with a non-judgmental attitude, gently bringing your focus back to the breath.

Recognize that the Mind will naturally drift away from the breath repeatedly.

And with gentle persistence, you may bring your attention back to the breath repeatedly, over and over again.

As we approach the end of this session, slowly open your eyes. Take a moment to observe and acknowledge how you are feeling in this present moment.

Let us celebrate and congratulate ourselves for dedicating this time to nurturing our well-being and for choosing a path that leads to holistic growth and wellness.

Once again, thank you for your time and dedication. Until then take care and stay tuned

See you all in our next session, and get ready for an enriching journey ahead.

CHAPTER 4
Enjoy the Mindful Coffee Moments

Mindfulness is a practice that makes us aware of our presence in the current moment, carrying the same awareness to the next moment, and the next moment that follows. As we enter next future moment, it becomes a present moment, and this present moment slips into the past. Mindfulness gives full awareness of every passing moment.

Through conscious practice of mindfulness, we become better versions of ourselves and gear our lives to handle stress in a better way aiding to make careful choices and regulate our responses rather than reacting.

As we include mindfulness practice in our everyday life, we start getting better at making our choices, our responses become wiser and eventually, we keep discovering new dimensions of mindfulness along the way.

Informal mindfulness can be practiced anytime, anywhere. Whether we are cooking, eating, waiting for an elevator, or traveling on a busy subway, there are no restrictions to practicing mindfulness.

In fact, these moments provide the perfect opportunity for a short mindfulness session.

During such times, we can consciously engage our senses with the present moment and our surroundings, including all the noises and the various thoughts and feelings we may be experiencing.

To start, we can try a brief mindfulness exercise while warming a cup of coffee or tea. We might call these moments 'Mindful Coffee Moments.'

Warming up a cup of coffee for 45 seconds in the microwave is an excellent starting point for casual mindfulness practice. As the timer counts down and your coffee warms up, observe how the cup revolves on the tray. Listen to the gentle hum of the microwave.

These 'Mindful Coffee Moments' anchor our attention and tie us to the Present Moment, we consciously watch these moments with full awareness, and in these moments, we may bring our awareness towards our breath.

Those 45 seconds become an excellent mindfulness practice if you simply stay present, moment by moment.

Adore its flavor; notice the sensations that arise within you with each sip, and feel the warmth as you hold the cup in your hands. Smell the rich aroma of the coffee. Notice the freshness and the feeling of relaxation that you are experiencing.

While relishing the coffee, you may take some moments to express gratitude for these wonderful moments.

Gratitude comes with its own benefits.

We may enjoy the mindfulness moments in almost every aspect of our daily lives.

Let's try to perform some of our basic activities with full awareness. To begin with, let's take our first activity of the day- Brushing your Teeth.

Notice how you apply the paste to the brush, how you hold the brush, feel the contact of the brush with your teeth, gum, or tongue. Watch how you feel a tingling sensation, the freshness. We may step-by-step breakdown this activity furthermore into finer segments by bringing attention to the movement of the wrist, notice how our lips adjust voluntarily during different phases of brushing. Observe the lips when brushing the front teeth or shifting to the rear teeth and while brushing the teeth at the very back of the mouth. Once done brushing, try to take a mindful shower. It will appear as if you are doing these activities for the first time.

It will be an astonishing experience to know that these simple daily activities are so well coordinated.

At first glance brushing teeth appears to be simply scrubbing teeth, but when we precisely observe the sequence of actions, the coordination of movements between the wrist, lips, tongue, we realise that we have been doing these activities for a lifetime but never realized that we have been gifted with a fascinating, well-coordinated and complex system. We get a holistic experience when we connect our bodily activities to the Mind.

You can extend your scope by taking a shower. Notice the flow of water, the temperature of the water when it comes into contact with your body, the sensations that arise and so on.

"The present moment is the most precious moment-a moment that aligns you with your future and helps to reclaim your inner balance."

Taking care of this present moment is the most remarkable stepping stone for the next moment.

Nurturing this present moment is the most effective stepping stone towards creating the next moment.

Trying to forcefully control the thoughts only creates more internal conflict, heightens anxiety, and leave us more vulnerable and weakens our ability to face going challenges of life.

On the contrary, when we recognize and notice our emotions and accept our suffering without resistance, it eases our life. Accepting our own thoughts non-judgementally makes all the difference.

Resource:

Mindfulness Session 3:
Holistic way of living

Welcome to this session of Mindfulness practice.

The only time truly available to us is right now.

Let's utilize these few moments for ourselves, (brief pause), a few moments for our own well-being. Find a quiet but comfortable place where you won't be disturbed.

Make yourself comfortable, and take a dignified posture, it does not matter whether you are sitting, standing or lying down.

Close your eyes gently, and take your time to settle in.

Check in on your posture.

Take a moment to observe if any sensations arising within your body, any pain or discomfort at this moment.

You may make necessary adjustments to your posture as required.

Begin by taking a few deep breaths in and exhaling slowly, focusing on your breath.

Mindfulness practice will help us establish a connection between mind and body, and will help bring our attention to the present moment.

Breathing will remain the primary focus of attention in this session and all other sessions that follow.

Mindfulness is an acquirable skill that can be developed through practice, similar to any other skill, mindfulness requires dedication, persistence, and patience.

Bring your attention to the sensations of breathing, specifically in the area where the breath is most prominent or distinct for you, which can be the gentle movement of the air flowing through your nostrils, or the rhythmic rise and fall of your chest, or the subtle expansion and contraction of your belly.

Allow your attention to rest on the breath, and with each breath you inhale and exhale, visualize the vital life-energy flowing throughout your body.

Let's keep ourselves aware of the breath in these moments and during periods of silence.

(brief pause)

Open your eyes gently, and see how you are feeling.

Let us congratulate ourselves for taking this time, recognizing the importance of this moment and for making a conscious decision to choose a progressive path toward holistic growth and wellness. See you all in our next session.

CHAPTER 5
Practice of mindfulness

The essence of Beauty lies in simplicity, as it reflects clarity and authenticity.

A simple way to understand mindfulness is to look at the world as it is, looking at the things as they are, looking at the events as they are, looking at the thoughts as they arise, without making any judgment, with pure acceptance.

Mindfulness is more about understanding and respecting the power of the Mind.

We don't try to suppress our thoughts or try to control or manipulate the thoughts, rather, we discern the mind with curiosity, observe its natural flow.

Our thoughts come and go like waves, sometimes in the form of small waves, causing ripples and sometimes they come like mighty waves, sweeping away our awareness and drowning us in the ocean of emotions and uncertainty.

All waves are bound to go through a life cycle of originating, reaching the peak and vanishing and being replaced by new waves that emerge and vanish again, irrespective of their magnitude and size.

Observing a thought at its inception by noticing its formation, rising and calming. As we observe the formation of thoughts, and the emotions associated with those thoughts.

We train ourselves to observe the thoughts and emotions as a seeker, as a Seer. This is a skill, and an art that can be learned, acquired, and elevated.

"Mindfulness gathers the scattered kinetic energy of the wandering mind and condenses it into a unified potential- the quiet power of awakened consciousness."

The untrained mind is rarely still. It moves from thought to thought, memory to memory, anticipation to anticipation. This constant movement is like kinetic energy- active, restless, always in motion. The mind jumps, reacts, compares, judges, and imagines. Energy is continuously spent.

When we practice mindfulness, we do not fight this movement. We observe it.

In observation, something subtle begins to happen. The scattered motion of thought starts to slow. Instead of being pulled in many directions, attention begins to collect. What was dispersed becomes gathered.

Just as flowing water can be channeled to create power, the wandering energy of the mind- when gently directed through awareness- transforms. It is no longer wasted in reaction. It becomes stored as potential.

This potential is not tension. It is not suppressive.

It is an immense reservoir of absolute awareness.

In physics, potential energy is energy held in position- stable, ready, grounded. In mindfulness, this "position" is the present moment. When attention rests here, energy is conserved. It is no longer leaking into regret of the past or anxiety about the future.

The mind shifts from scattered movement to centered presence.

This is the focused flow of energy. Energy is not eliminated. It is gathered and unified.

In this state, consciousness is not dull or passive. It is alert, steady, and ready- like a calm lake that clearly reflects the sky.

Mindfulness does not reduce the power of the mind, rather, it transforms restless motion into conscious potential.

Every living species has a capability to be Mindful; to connect their body and mind, the degree or capacity of their Mindfulness doesn't matter. It is a continuous and genuine wish to learn and practice.

Mindfulness is often described as awareness of the present moment, without reacting. It is an art, a practice, and on top of that, mindfulness is not passive. It requires an ardent quality, a keen desire, a steady flame of enthusiasm and sincerity that keeps awareness alive.

Mindfulness is often paired with qualities such as clear comprehension and ardent effort. To be ardent in mindfulness means caring deeply about each moment with a keen desire for mindfulness practice.

It is not simply noticing one's breath, steps, or thoughts in a detached way, rather, it is attending to them with genuine devotion and a burning desire to experience the fullness of life as it unfolds.

Without ardency, mindfulness becomes a passive exercise, a lifeless daily routine.

"With a touch of ardency, mindfulness transforms from a technical skill to a way of life, making us move closer to the Riches of Life."

To eat mindfully is not only to taste food, but to honor it. To walk mindfully is not only to move, but to be fully alive with each step.

When nurtured properly, it provides warmth, light, and protection. Likewise, ardency in practice is gentle but firm. It sustains awareness through joy and through difficulty, helping one face suffering with courage and clarity.

In daily life, cultivating ardent mindfulness means meeting each experience with openness and care. The ordinary is no longer dismissed as trivial, because every sound, every breath, and every encounter is seen as part of the living present. To live this way is to affirm that life itself is precious.

To practice mindfulness ardently is to keep the inner flame alive, illuminating both the silence within and the vast pastures of awareness in which the mind may rest.

We will try to practice small sessions for

- Mindfulness of Body and Posture
- Mindfulness of Breath
- Mindfulness of Feelings
- Mindfulness of Thoughts:

Just notice the thoughts without being judgmental or flowing with the thoughts. There is a difference between flowing along with the thoughts and observing the thoughts.

In daily life, cultivating ardent mindfulness means meeting each experience with openness and care. The ordinary is no longer dismissed as trivial, because every sound, every breath, and every encounter is seen as part of the living present. To live this way is to affirm that life itself is precious.

Resource:

Mindfulness Session 4:
Mindfulness of Sensations (part 1)

Welcome to another session of mindfulness practice.

Let's begin our session by expressing gratitude for being present in this moment.

To begin with, take a comfortable posture, ensuring that your back is straight yet relaxed.

Take a few deep breaths.

Experience each incoming breath and each outgoing breath consciously.

Now, let's bring your attention to your jaw.

Notice whether your jaw is clenched or relaxed. Take a moment to simply be aware of the sensations that arise in this area.

Now, expand your awareness to encompass your entire face.

Take a moment to fully experience and acknowledge the sensations that may arise.

You may notice tingling, tightness, a feeling of relaxation or even no sensation at all.

Embrace whatever you are experiencing in this moment, cultivating a non-reactive attitude.

Stay fully present and immerse yourself in these sensations for a while.

You can fully appreciate and engage with the present moment.

By nurturing a non-judgmental awareness, experiencing the depth and richness of each sensation.

Now, open your eyes gently and observe how you are feeling.

Congratulations on completing this short session of mindfulness. Thank you for joining us, and we look forward to having you in the next session.

Till then, take care and stay tuned.

SECTION
II

CHAPTER 6
Noticing the Turbulence within

Understanding Mental and Emotional Turbulence

Have you ever noticed the turbulence happening in your mind?

At times, we feel restless, and thoughts rush in from all directions, filling the mind with internal conflicts and emotional turmoil. You might enter a stage of emotional turbulence, where it's difficult to control the storm of anger, anxiety, guilt, or frustration.

The shift happens the moment you notice and realize, "Ah, this is turbulence- just turbulence." Something shifts. Instead of getting caught in the turbulence, you start watching the commotion.

Am I trapped in the trench of trance? (Brach, 2020)

Trance may be understood as a state of mind when a person becomes disconnected with the present moment and drifts away in their own thoughts, realistically the person gets dragged in the trench of emotions, gets trapped in the trench of trance.

It is like living life in an Auto-Pilot mode, where you do not have any control.

As the emotion grows, the trench of trance widens and the person gets carried away into a deep, altered state of mind, and very quickly the person becomes trapped in their own thoughts.

The awareness of surroundings gets faded.

Thoughts and emotions are deeply intertwined and keep fuelling each other.

A thought can trigger an emotion, and emotions reinforce the thought further, intensifying the emotions.

This can be well understood by a simple daily example. The moment you have a thought of failing, your body starts reacting before you even notice, you start feeling tightness in your chest or butterflies in your stomach, and you start feeling anxious at the same moment.

On the flip side, when we feel that we are well-prepared and can handle the situation, we feel confident and calm.

This all starts with Knowing. Knowing and allowing your thoughts to flow freely lets the tide of emotions rise and fall, say **Yes** and accept them as they are.

Thoughts and emotions feed each other and form a loop that keeps on going. The thought-emotion loop has a dynamic relationship.

The moment you realize that you are getting trapped in the trench of trance, you break the cycle by stopping the fuel to your mind, shutting down the fuel of memories, cutting off the fuel of emotions. Lack of fuel would stop the automatic spiral and surface you out of trance.

There are certain Indicators of being trapped in the trench of trance. Check within yourself.

Do I occasionally get zoned out, and become unresponsive?

Do I get distracted easily? Do I easily lose track of time?

Have I ever finished a packet of chips or popcorn unknowingly, without realizing?

Do I ever get stuck with my phone scrolling reels for hours?

Resource:

Mindfulness Session 5: Embracing RAIN for Inner Well-being ~ inspired by Tara Brach

When you feel down, anxious, or stressed, employ mindfulness as a remedy using the four-step method called 'RAIN.'

RAIN is an acronym representing the four steps:

'R' stands for Recognize- recognize what you are going through, acknowledging the rising and falling.

"levels of anxiety, feelings, and thoughts."

Letter "A" stands for Accept, to accept what is happening inside. Exert no resistance.

Allow yourself to feel the way you are feeling, with no judgment, "It's okay to feel this way."

Letter "I" stands for Investigate.

Investigate and explore why you feel that way.

Ask yourself, "What's going on here? Why do I feel like this?"

Letter "N" stands for Nurture.

Nurture yourself by giving a gentle hug. Be kind, treating yourself as you would have treated a friend in a tough time.

Nurture your feelings and express, "I care about you, and you deserve some kindness."

As you massage and nurture the stressed or anxious part of your body, send a gentle message inward to the anxious aspect, acknowledging its presence with compassion.

This nurturing approach is a vital element of self-compassion.

We will explore self-compassion further in upcoming sessions.

RAIN acts as an umbrella for your emotions, aiding you in weathering the storm with mindfulness and self-compassion.

In moments of challenge, embrace mindfulness as a supportive friend. Allow the 'RAIN' method to guide you.

This meditation technique originates from Buddhist teachings and has been adapted and articulated by Tara Brach, a renowned international author and mindfulness instructor.

Thank you for joining us, and we look forward to having you in the next session.

See you all in our next session.

Anxiety:-

Ever since I accepted a new position at work, my days have been starting with anxiety, and most of the time ended with me blaming myself, considering that I may not be competent enough to handle this position. That feeling would trigger anxiety and stress.

I am sure there are many others like me whose days begin with stress and unease.

Every one of us would agree that there are so many unspoken expectations and commitments at any workplace or broadly speaking, true to any relationships and every aspect of life.

We work so hard to fulfill these commitments and stand up to the expectations, all these efforts to meet the work requirements and to keep healthy and harmonious relations.

But there are times when the expectation cannot be

met, or there are times when the expectation bar gets raised and many times the expectation bar keeps on rising. That leaves us with a feeling of inadequacy.

Mental events consume lots of mental energy and inner landscape.

Human bodies are designed to react to a situation by entering fight-or-flight mode, but if a person is continuously gripped by the perceived threat, then this situation needs to be addressed.

As a matter of fact, many of us are doing highly demanding jobs, way more demanding than our bearing capacity, this is escalating stress levels in humans. Our bodies are not designed to withstand the excessive stress for prolonged periods of time.

Profound changes come in our lives as we start learning how to respond reasonably instead of reacting spontaneously to a situation.

A few years back, my nephew was suffering from anxiety and panic attacks. It all started with small signs, like hesitating to speak in class, he had to challenge himself hard to make eye contact with teachers. He would get anxious while getting ready for school, while submitting an assignment and even while travelling for school. His heart started pounding fast, and a few times he got dizzy while travelling in the school bus.

At one point, his anxiety got too intense that it started interfering with his daily performance.

Thankfully, he received a Mindfulness-Based Cognitive Therapy (MBCT), which helped him to manage his symptoms. Through guided sessions, he learned to observe his thoughts, learned to recognize his feelings as soon as he started getting anxious. He also learned to take control over his anxiety and learned the mechanism to cope with anxiety.

Mindfulness as a First Responder to Anxiety and Depression.

Mindfulness is a powerful tool for combating anxiety and depression. It acts like a first responder to anxiety and governs anxiety when the mind begins to spiral into fear or hopelessness. Mindfulness invites us to take a different attitude toward our emotions. Instead of running away from them or drowning in them, we learn to observe them with awareness and compassion. Through mindfulness, we begin to notice the constant flow of our thoughts and feelings. It teaches us to identify the negative patterns that fuel anxiety and low mood, and gently brings our attention back to the present moment- the only place where peace truly exists.

Nothing transforms overnight. The journey through anxiety or depression is not a straight path. There are days when progress feels visible- moments when we think, yes, things are finally getting better- and then there are days when everything feels like a setback. This is natural. Healing unfolds gradually, much like how dawn slowly replaces the night.

In this journey, mindfulness becomes both a guide and a companion. Gradually, as awareness deepens, confidence begins to return. I remember how my nephew began to engage more- speaking to classmates again, participating in class activities, and gradually rediscovering his sense of self.

With continuous practice, patience, and the willingness to stay with the process, he eventually found a balance. Mindfulness helped him rebuild inner stability and confidence. Even today, he continues to rely on mindfulness- not as a quick fix, but as a way of living, a daily practice that keeps him grounded and connected to the present.

He still uses the mindfulness techniques to manage his stress.

Anxiety and fear are the basic emotions present in

each one of us. Moderate anxiety and fear are helpful and essential for our survival.

It is important to note that the anxiety cannot be eliminated entirely, but something fundamentally changes. The anxiety can no longer take control over us, instead we learn to shift our attention from the narrative that is building in our mind to actual experience in our body and heart.

Simply ask yourself 'What am I feeling right now', or ask yourself 'What is going on inside me right now'.

If you are feeling distressed, register that feeling as Distress. If you are experiencing anxiety, register that feeling as Anxiety.

Simply know that feeling, recognize it, and allow your emotions to flow in with no arguments, or judgments. Be receptive towards your feelings with openness and compassion.

The thought-emotion loop has a dynamic relationship. Our mind behaves like a fluid, seamlessly flowing between its Conscious realm and the Unconscious realm. The mind effortlessly swings between the moments, at times, the mind feels joyous, filled with fantasies and dreams, at other moments the mind may get filled with fear and anxiety. Sometimes the mind gets frustrated and sometimes gets lost in fantasies. It is important to recognize that there are no boundaries set on the mind and it has a remarkable agility.

As soon as you realize that the mind is getting trapped in the trenches of trance, take a brief pause, pull your mind back to the surface

Experiment at times when you realize that you've been trapped in the trench of trance, bring your mind back to the surface and use a technique called 'PEACE'.

PEACE-a simple technique to connect to the present moment and ground the mind, out of the trench.

I recall that while waiting for my turn at a cash counter of a grocery store, the person standing ahead of me had a handful of coupons and flyers for price matching.

Next to this person was a lady who wasn't just smiling; she was genuinely admiring the effort they were making to save money.

I wondered how someone could stay so calm and admire that.

Meanwhile, I was growing increasingly frustrated, getting impatient with all this price matching business. Impulsively, I switched to a different checkout lane. I felt so relieved to leave that lane and I was convinced that I had made the right decision. But soon after, I noticed that other lines were moving faster than the one I had switched to, and a familiar cycle of restlessness kicked in. I found myself scanning other aisles, trying to justify my choice.

My wife, who was standing beside me, noticed me getting agitated, gently reminded me to stay calm, and told me to simply observe what was happening around me.

All my turbulence vanished for a moment when I realized, why was I rushing? Was there any reason to rush, or was that just a part of me?

I took a pause and started a brief mindfulness session, focusing on my breath.

Later I decided to take some time for mindfulness practice

PEACE.

(P) -Pause	Pause and ground yourself to the Present moment. Ask yourself how am I feeling right now? Am I feeling anxious?

(E)-Examine	Examine what is arising within your body and mind? Direct your attention towards parts where you may feel tightness or numbness. Investigate what you feel most difficult. Are you feeling any discomfort or feel the pounding of your heart? Continue investigating the pulls and pushes arising in your mind due to any underlying fear, uncertainty, or guilt, consciously.
(A)-Accept	Accepting your Feelings as they are. Acceptance invites us to fully experience whatever we are confronting, without judgment. The practice involves breathing mindfully and allowing your feelings to unfold naturally. Whether you are experiencing tension, discomfort or irritation, simply notice it, acknowledge that it is present and allow it to be.
(C)-Compassionately Nurture	Compassionately Nurture yourself, responding with compassion, kindness and support that you need at that moment.
(E)-Engage	Engage yourself with the next moment, with a feeling of gratitude that you got an opportunity to experience and embrace the moments as they unfold.

The **PEACE** technique worked perfectly for me and just in 30 seconds I was able to get rid of my restlessness.

When we start watching the Present moment, it reflects a deeper inquiry into the nature of consciousness and self-awareness. We start becoming aware of our thoughts, feelings and emotions. We begin to become aware of our awareness. We see that thoughts and feelings arise and vanish, followed by new thoughts, feelings and perceptions.

Our unconscious mind is always busy on the back end of our mind.

It is busy building stories, plans and fantasies. It is holding a vast reservoir of memories, many of which remain beyond the awareness of our conscious mind.

On the other hand, our conscious mind operates on the front end; while functioning at the forefront, it also communicates with the unconscious mind.

Resource:

Mindfulness Session 6: Mindfulness of thoughts & feelings (Part-1)

Welcome to another session of mindfulness practice.

In this session, we will explore the dynamics between Thoughts and Feelings.

As discussed in our previous session, thoughts play a crucial role in various mental activities, such as generating ideas, forming beliefs, and interpreting information.

From a psychological perspective, actively engaging in these mental activities results in the continuous shaping and refining of our thoughts, which significantly contributes to our overall mental functioning and behavior.

"Thoughts serve as the driving force behind shaping our emotions, generating positive or negative interpretations of situations.

Similarly, emotions also impact our thoughts."

The dynamic relationship between thoughts and emotions significantly contributes to the overall subjective experience of our lives.

Let's start our session by mindfully taking a few mindful deep breaths. Take a slow and deep inhalation, followed by a gentle and complete exhalation. Close your eyes gently, take a dignified posture, and fully embrace the present moment.

As we settle into this state, let's direct our awareness towards any thoughts that may be floating in the background of your mind.

During this practice, you may have noticed thoughts arising in the mind space, lingering momentarily, and then vanishing, only to be replaced by new thoughts that emerge. It's essential to observe this natural flow of thoughts without getting attached to them, allowing them to come and go freely.

Imagine these passing thoughts as clouds gently drifting through the unbounded sky of your mind's landscape.

Through practicing mindfulness, we learn to observe our thoughts, recognize their patterns, and avoid becoming entangled in them.

CHAPTER 7
Introducing the CALM Practice

(Connect Consciously with Curiosity, Acknowledge/Allow/Accept, Listen to your inner experience/ Loosen grip/ Let Go, Meet yourself Mindfully with compassion & Nurture)

There are moments when the mind feels trapped, lost in its trenches of worry and confusion. The more we try to silence it or fight our way out, the deeper we sink.

Peace cannot be attained by force, but it unfolds through awareness.

I began using a simple inner reminder, a practice I call CALM.

CALM is a practice to turn reaction into reflection, tension into tenderness. CALM is the practice that pulls us out of the trenches of trance to the surface of awareness. CALM practice helps allow the breath to become a gentle bridge back to safety, rather, we keep forcing ourselves to achieve tranquility.

C- Consciously, connect to the present moment with Curiosity.

Consciously, connect to the present moment.

Notice your breath, the sensations in your body, the areas of tightness- without trying to change them. This anchors you in the present moment and interrupts mental resistance. Pause and gently bring your attention to physical sensations.

Feel the contact of your body with the chair on which you are sitting, or the ground beneath your feet, feel the movement of air flowing in through your nostrils. Consciously connecting to the present moment is the entry point to recognize what is happening inside me right now?

What sensations are most obvious and where they are most noticeable? Curiosity invites us to examine our experiences.

A- Allow-Acknowledge-Accept

Allow yourself to feel what you are feeling right now. Let the experience be exactly as it is.

Instead of pushing pain away or denying it, gently allow the feelings to come to the surface. Allowing does not mean liking the pain; it means stopping the struggle against it.

Take every breath mindfully and allow your feeling to unfold freely, even though you may not like those feelings to come out. Whatever you are experiencing in this moment, give permission to unfold.

Whether it is tension, irritation, or a quiet discomfort-simply notice it.

Acknowledge that it's here and allow it to be.

Awareness is always the first step toward softening and eventually releasing whatever we are holding.

The intention is to let your feelings flow freely with no resistance and gently ask yourself

"What am I feeling right now?" Is it anger, fear, regret or grief?

"What emotions am I feeling?"

Feel it, experience it

"Where is it most noticeable?"

"Is it in the stomach or feeling some pressure in the chest?"

"Are there any sensations on face?"

Let the emotions flow in, rather than, without judging them, allow them as they are, with no judgement or guilt. Accept your experiences as they are.

Acceptance does not mean giving up on your circumstances. It simply means acknowledging what is present in this moment, the experience that is happening in the moment.

When we start allowing the experience as it is, radical acceptance helps restrain the formation of a spiral of negative thoughts, it curbs it at its very origination before it grows.

L- Listen to your inner experience- Loosen Grip-Let Go

Listen to your inner experience with kindness, openness and curiosity. Gently **turn inward and notice** what feels most difficult in this moment.

Loosen the inner grip, instead of resisting, try to locate the part of your body where the sensations are most noticeable. Allow it to be as it is.

Listen to your sensations mindfully, and if possible, do not try to fix your experience.

Continue the practice at your own pace, unless something feels severe or requires immediate assistance.

Sensations are a way to communicate with us, listen to the signals. Let the tension melt and give permission to release your stress and anxiety.

Every emotion carries information, slowly scan yourself from within.

Notice if the rhythm of your breath is still normal, or has it changed?

How are you feeling right now?

Does my body feel the same, or do I notice sensations like palpitations, heart beating faster?

Which part of my body is involved the most?

Just listen with curiosity and awareness.

M- Meet yourself with compassion & Mindfully Nurture with kindness and understanding.

This is where healing begins. When you meet your experience with warmth rather than resistance, awareness naturally opens, and calm arises from within.

The CALM practice is not about suppressing emotions or forcing positivity; it is about creating a space wide enough for experiences to unfold naturally, a space where thoughts and feelings can be seen with clarity, held with compassion, and gently guided back to center through conscious choices.

Your choice reveals who you are. You have a choice to take control of yourself, to control your feelings, the deep inside feelings.

Life is all about dilemmas and choices. Reject it or accept it. It is your life and your choice. Both are acceptable. Open yourself and learn to make yourself stronger, stronger from the inside. In the moments of dilemma, Mindfulness is our survival kit in this chaotic world. Mindfulness is not merely a great way of life or a great ideal, but it is a practice, it is a discipline and indeed a strong commitment to yourself.

The world is filled with impulses and responses, diversity of behaviours. We come across a pattern of actions and reactions, everywhere.

Things and situations may change surprisingly and put us in jeopardy. We cannot control every situation, but we can choose how we meet them with awareness, balance, and compassion.

Mindfulness gently invites us to pause before

reacting, encompasses how to react to a given problem and how to get back to your life.

Mindfulness is not an escape from challenges but a way to meet them with presence.

Engaging mindfulness in our daily lives and incorporating it into our lifestyle.

In this awareness lies the true freedom to live consciously and fully in each unfolding moment.

Resource:

Mindfulness Session 7:
Mindful Practice- Anytime, Anywhere

Informal mindfulness can be practiced anywhere at any time.

Whether we are cooking, eating, waiting for an elevator, or in a subway, these moments provide an opportunity for a short mindfulness session.

During such times, consciously engage your senses with your current surroundings, thoughts and feelings.

For instance, while drinking, you can utilize these moments as a brief mindfulness session,

Feeling the warmth of the cup...

Appreciating the rich aroma... &

Noticing the awakening sensation with each sip...

Enjoy these beautiful moments and let gratitude flow.

Be aware of the environment around you.

It's a way of grounding yourself in the Now-Moments, rather than being caught up in the thoughts about the past or future

This informal mindfulness practice contributes to a more conscious and intentional way of living, fostering a sense of clarity, calmness and appreciation for the nuances of daily life

Thank you for joining this session and many more sessions to come.

Take care of yourself and stay tuned.

CHAPTER 8
Meet Yourself with Warmth

"You yourself, deserve your love and affection as much as anybody in the entire universe."

-Inspired by Buddha's teachings-

Imagine a scenario:

One fine morning you received a call from your friend.

"Hey... How are you doing? Is everything okay? you ask, but you sense something is off."

There's a pause on the other end- then an anxious and choked voice replies,

"Terrible... I have lost a lot of money in a single bet... everything I had built.

It was perfect timing, everything lined up, but then the market suddenly plunged... and, all my money vanished. I feel deeply disappointed and lost."

Now visualize your response as something like this:

"Well, I told you not to do that. Never put all your eggs in the same basket, but you never listened to me.

Now suffer the consequences."

Would you ever speak this way to someone you genuinely care about?

Of course not.

If this were a real friend in pain, you would try to listen to their pain, soften your tone, and with your heart filled with empathy. You would rather, try to calm them down. You would speak from the heart.

You would probably say something like:

"I know this deeply hurts. I am sorry you are going through this. It must feel like a huge setback, but please know that I am always there for you.

Everyone makes mistakes. We are all human. This hurts now, but this does not define you. You are more than this moment. You are resilient and will come back stronger."

That is compassion. That is how we naturally respond to our close ones.

But there arise some basic questions that need to be addressed:

Under similar circumstances, would you be treating yourself the same way you treat your loved ones?

Why do we hesitate to offer the same support to ourselves as we offer to our loved ones?

Why do we turn back to ourselves, become critical, cold and punishing?

Why do we extend patience, forgiveness, and understanding to friends and loved ones, and on the contrary, meet ourselves with criticism, impatience, and unrealistic expectations?

The first step of meeting yourself with warmth and care is "knowing." ***Know thyself.***

When we start seeing our sufferings and meet them face to face, gently and mindfully, we recognize what is truly happening within us. In that realization, we start accepting our experiences and our vulnerabilities, as they are. We turn more gentler toward the shortcomings, meet them with warmth and care, rather than being judgmental.

We start directing our attention inward, softening the

blockades we have built around our hearts, and that is when we say:

"I am hurting myself right now."

"I made a mistake, but I am also a human being."

"I can get through this, though that might not be easy."

"This is a moment of struggle, but I will overcome."

"This is a moment of struggle, and it will pass."

Knowing brings a core shift in perception toward us.

The word Healthy in its true sense can be understood as **'Heal' & 'Thy'**; literally meaning to Heal Yourself; heal your wounds- **"Heal-Thy."**

The **"Heal-Thy"** approach is about creating a safe inner space where experiences are allowed to unfold. Within this space emotions can be seen with clarity, held with Compassion and Care.

As our understanding of **"Heal-Thy"** deepens, the feeling of self-compassion and self-care grows, we start seeing a need for loving-kindness and care towards ourselves.

Self-compassion is **Heal-Thy**- to heal yourself by turning attention inward with intention of self-care.

Heal-Thy begin with a gentle inward shift, by listening to our inner voice, moving away from self-criticism, and treating ourselves with kindness, warmth and understanding, instead of analyzing ourself and criticizing.

Through Self-compassion and self-care, we gently turn to our truth. A friendly inner attitude begins to replace our self-criticism with self-support, cultivating a friendly attitude, rather than becoming our own inner enemy. This shift gives a balance and clear vision to see our painful feelings and thoughts with the same warmth that we would offer a friend.

We are always seeking ways to feel safe and protected. Our brains have evolved in such a way that many of our basic instincts still exist, dominating our behavior and influencing our actions.

Our brain often acts in a way that it must protect us. Brain feels obligated to provide protection from all threats that occur in our life-whether real and perceived. This protective behavior of our brain brings existence first over anything else. Whether we are standing in a social gathering, or going through financial insecurity, or a pre-emptive strike to save our self-image, brain will trigger its survival mode.

When a threat is sensed, our biological threat-defense system responds automatically to cope the situation by an immediate respond by switching to "fight, flight or freeze" mode. This functionality is activated by releasing stress hormones resulting in increased heart rate, blood pressure, and energy, getting us ready for confrontation or escape.

In the current ages, one of the most common threats we face is not from outside, but "The threat arising from within, the constant need to protect our self-image". We are afraid of looking weak and imperfect. We do not want to be seen as a loser. Minor mistakes such as typos can trigger a survival response. To protect ourselves from these imaginary threats, we build a shield of self-criticism with a belief that being self-critical prevents us from external judgments, thus protecting us from being judged by others.

Self-criticism is survival tactic, to avoid the future criticism. It is often our first response from within, arising to meet our need of remaining relevant and acceptable. Self-blaming gives an illusion of having things under control and we are trying to prevent any future risk of being fired or punished. This human pattern remained engraved within us. This is natural protection mechanism designed to keep us relevant, and safeguard against rejection and exclusion. Same survival instincts are still rooted within us even though we are no longer hunting for survival anymore, rather, working in office spaces and corporate environments.

A unique thing happens when we criticize ourselves- we begin attacking ourselves, while simultaneously we try to take refuge from the very attack. We become both-an Attacker and the one who is being Attacked-the aggressor and the defender.

Self-criticism is constantly evaluating us, counting our mistakes, flaws, and shortcomings and showing no sympathy. These threats, whether real or imaginary, put huge stress on our bodies and mind.

This negative self-judgment leads to feelings of guilt, inadequacy, shame, and psychological distress like anxiety and depression.

And when we finally make a call for self-compassion, through awareness and the CALM practice, something inside begins to shift.

This isn't just about feeling better; it's about seeing more clearly. Kindness allows us to look at us.

Lives mindfully, without distortion or panic.

As we soften inwardly, we learn to embrace ourselves as we are- to accept life as it is, and, to trust in our own quiet resilience, even with all our human flaws. This shift in the way we relate to ourselves changes everything. Life becomes less of a battle and more of a relationship rooted in care.

Self-compassion and self-care begin with a gentle shift- **softening the barriers** we have built around our own hearts. These walls once made us feel safe. They protected us from criticism, loneliness, and the exhausting pressure of appearing perfect. We built them because, at some point, it was the only way we knew how to survive.

But when we start turning toward ourselves with

kindness, the landscape changes. We stop hiding ourselves behind those walls of self-humiliation and self-criticism, rather, we begin to looking at our lives with a softer and understanding view, looking at our hardships, our struggles and our efforts. This shift provides comfort and self-respect.

It is the thought that truly counts. Each thought carries a signal, pointing us toward a deeper understanding of its intention. Thoughts are not merely fleeting ideas; they act as roadmaps- guiding the reconstruction of the self on the Heal-Thy journey, a journey toward self-care and self-healing.

Through self-compassion, Heal-Thy gently reveals where we stand, how we perceive our worth, and how willing we are to meet ourselves with kindness.

It shows us not who we should become, but how softly we are able to be present with who we already are.

In that those mindful moments of **self-compassion and self-care**, we start thinking with a positive attitude towards ourselves:

Self-Criticism Thoughts- Negative Emotions	**Shift towards Positive Thoughts- Heal-Thy**
I am behind, I am not adequate, something is wrong with me.	This is my journey; this is my life.
This shouldn't be happening.	Ups and downs are part of life.
Something is wrong with me, I don't deserve any care.	I am human and I deserve care and love.
I am not strong enough to handle this, I am finished.	I can come back and will come back stronger.

As we slowly learn to embrace ourselves- our flaws,

our fears, our mistakes and everything in between us, we uncover a quiet resilience within us: the strength to allow us to grow and evolve despite our imperfections.

The Transformation That Begins with Self-Kindness

Through self-compassion and self-care, we become gentler with ourselves in the very places where we were once rigid, harsh, or uncaring. Instead of fighting our imperfections, we begin to hold them with patience. Instead of criticizing our struggles, we start to understand them. This softening is not weakness; it is a powerful acknowledgment of our shared humanity- an understanding that we are not alone in our pain, that suffering and imperfection are universal threads that connect us all.

As we learn to accept our shortcomings and embrace our imperfections, a quiet transformation unfolds. We start treating ourselves with the same care we offer others. We approach our inner world with humility, kindness, and presence. And, slowly, the tone of our inner life begins to change.

Psychologically, self-compassion and self-care rest on three interconnected components, where each component supports the others.

The Three Core Components of self-compassion and self-care as summarized by researcher Dr. Kristin Neff: (Kristin Neff, 2018)

Self-Kindness	Being warm, gentle and supportive toward oneself rather than harshly self-critical and judgmental
Common Humanity	Recognizing that imperfection, flaws, and suffering are a shared part of human experience, which reduces feeling of isolation and inadequacy
Mindfulness	Being aware of one's difficult emotions and thoughts

When we make a mistake, we don't just feel bad about what happened- we often feel disconnected. It's as if our suffering pushes us into a lonely corner, quietly whispering to ourselves: "It's just me... I'm the only one who feels this way."

But the moment we remind ourselves that pain is a universal human experience, something shifts within.

The pain you feel in your difficult moments is, in many ways, the same kind of hurt I feel in mine. Our circumstances may differ, the depth of pain may vary, our stories may not match. Reminding you that the essence of being human is shared:

We all struggle, we all stumble, we all get hurt, and we all heal.

Self-compassion and self-care transform suffering into a point of connection rather than separation. Recognizing this makes it easier to carry our pain and suffering.

We realize that we are not an exception, and certainly, we are not alone.

And this understanding becomes a powerful companion on the path of self-compassion and self-care.

Noticing painful thoughts and feelings with balance- neither suppressing them nor getting swept away by them.

These components work together to create a compassionate, grounded, and balanced relationship with ourselves.

Life changes altogether when we learn to meet ourselves with this blend of kindness, understanding, and common humanity. We stop being harsh and uncaring toward our own pain. We begin to acknowledge our shortcomings without tearing ourselves down. Our imperfections become reminders of our shared humanity, rather than reasons for shame.

Gradually, we start looking at our struggles with tenderness. We allow ourselves to be softer. We give ourselves permission to be human.

Mettā is a Pali word for Loving-Kindness as taught by Sharon Salzberg (Salzberg, 2020),

Loving-kindness ***(Mettā)*** is not about forcing positive feelings or being nice all the time. It is the steady intention to meet ourselves and others with care, warmth, and goodwill, exactly as we are.

At its core, the practice begins with self-compassion and **"Heal-Thy",** learning to offer ourselves kindness without judgment or conditions. From there, loving-kindness naturally extends outward: to loved ones, to difficult relationships, and eventually to all beings. This gradual expansion trains the heart to remain open rather than reactive.

Loving-kindness is a trainable skill, not a personality trait. Through simple phrases like "May I be safe. May you be peaceful," we re-educate the mind, softening fear, anger, and self-criticism. Over time, this practice strengthens emotional resilience, reduces stress, and nurtures a sense of connection and belonging.

Most importantly, loving-kindness does not deny pain or difficulty. Instead, it offers a way to stay present with life- without hardening.

Loving-kindness is the practice of befriending life. In the CALM approach, we Connect with ourselves just as we are, without needing to be fixed. We Allow kindness to replace judgment. We Listen to the heart's natural wish for safety, peace, and ease. And we Move forward with intention, extending that same goodwill outward- to loved ones, to neutral people, to difficult relationships, and eventually to all beings.

From a Heal-Thy perspective, loving-kindness begins within. It teaches us that healing does not come from harsh self-correction, but from learning to stay present without hardening.

As Sharon Salzberg teaches, loving-kindness is not forced positivity; it is a trainable quality of the heart. Through simple, repeated phrases-

May I be safe.

May you be peaceful.

The mind is gently re-educated. Fear softens, reactivity loosens, and resilience grows.

Loving-kindness does not remove pain from life. It changes how we relate to pain- meeting it with care instead of resistance, and with connection instead of isolation.

Guided practice/meditation

Begin by gently bringing your attention inward.

Connect with yourself just as you are in this moment.

There is nothing to fix.

Allow kindness to be present.

Let go of judgment, even briefly.

Listen to the heart's natural wish:

to be safe, to be peaceful, to be at ease.

Silently offer these phrases:

May I be safe.

May I be peaceful.

May I live with ease.

Notice how the body responds- without forcing anything.

When you're ready, let this kindness expand outward:

to someone you love,

to someone neutral,

to someone difficult,

and eventually to all beings.

Move forward gently, carrying this intention with you.

Loving-kindness does not erase pain.

It allows us to meet life as it is-

With care instead of resistance,

and with connection instead of isolation.

Heal-Thy begins with self-awareness, creates a safe shared space, honors differences, and values small moments of connection.

When **Heal-Thy** guides the intention, an intention to be friendly with self and **CALM** guides the response, inner noise softens into clarity.

Over time, this is no longer a technique. It becomes a way of living, being fully present with the mind, and compassionate toward the one experiencing it.

When CALM is practiced within the framework of Heal-Thy, conflict naturally shifts from reaction to reflection, and from division to understanding.

In this way, disagreements become opportunities to deepen trust, strengthen compassion, and nurture a more resilient relationship.

This is Heal-Thy and CALM, working together to restore balance, one mindful moment at a time.

To be truly healthy is to **Heal-Thy** -to turn inward with care before reaching outward.

Mindfulness invites a pause and a pause is the doorway to healing.

Heal-Thy begins when we meet our inner world with kindness, when we choose self-compassion over self-criticism, and presence in the moment over reaction.

CALM technique turns rigid mental exercise into a genuine healing process. With the practice of CALM, you become the person offering care and warmth to your own self.

Here is how to weave self-compassion into each layer of the CALM framework.

This is where CALM becomes practice.

C- Connect with Present Moment- activating your Care System with Heal-Thy

Take a Pause. Breathe with full awareness. Anchor yourself to the present moment.

Allow the breath to become a gentle bridge of friendship by deactivating the body's threat-defense system and activating your Care System- Heal-Thy.

A- Acknowledge and Allow

Notice what is arising of thoughts, emotions, sensations.

Noticing deepens into validating.

Name the feeling gently, without blame or resistance. "This is stress," or "This is a feeling of inadequacy."

Add a supportive truth: "This is a moment of suffering,"

Allow yourself to feel you as receiving blessings of loving kindness and the support of Self-care.

Acknowledge that these are your feelings and you are a recipient of Compassion and Care.

You may recite:

May I accept myself as I am.

May I forgive myself.

May I be strong.

May I be patient.

L- Listen

Listen deeply to your inner experience with Empathy. Listen as you would to someone you deeply care about. You would not rush them or ask them to be different. You would stay. Offer that same presence to your inner experience.

M- Move with Care- Protecting Your Dignity

Move with Care. Respond with intention. Choose actions and words that protect dignity- yours and others.

Ask, "What do I need right now to feel safe and respected?"

To meet suffering with awareness, validate it with kindness, listen without urgency, and respond in ways that protect your dignity.

This is Heal-Thy in practice.

Resource:

Mindfulness Session 8:
Mindfulness of sounds, thoughts & feelings (part 1)

Welcome to another session of mindful practice.

In this practice we will explore the power of thought.

As we begin our practice, establish yourself in this present moment.

Choose a comfortable but dignified posture. Close your eyes gently and bring your attention to the breath.

Now, let's direct our attention to the sense of hearing. Open yourself to the world of sounds that surround you.

Indeed, our surroundings are filled with a multitude of noises. Whether- It's the hum of air conditioners, the rumble of airplane engines, the beep of a microwave, or the cheerful chirping of birds.

We are constantly immersed in a symphony of sounds.

And being mindful of these diverse noises can help us, cultivate a deeper connection between body and mind.

Try to focus on the pure sensations of the sounds, their pitch, their texture, and their rhythm.

Be aware of the space from where the sound is sourced from. Notice for sounds within the sounds.

Let the sounds fade in the background and bring your attention to the thoughts.

Notice how easily distractions can come and how easily a sound can create stories and imaginations.

Let's conclude today's session with a statement-

It's truly remarkable how our minds can swiftly wander and create narratives in response to the sounds around us.

Thank you for joining this session and many more sessions to come.

We look forward to having you in many more sessions to come.

CHAPTER 9
Suffering to Self- Compassion- the CALM way

Living in pain is not easy. Do not expect anyone to fully understand your journey. Though many may walk beside you on this path, everyone has to go in solitude, this is a personal journey accompanied with pain and suffering, but within this solitude we can be befriended by healing and self-care-**"Heal-Thy."** True understanding of suffering belongs to one who is living it, living with it, and living in it. Others may offer support, comfort and sympathy, but the experience of pain itself is deeply personal and cannot be fully shared.

This is an endless marathon that you may have to cross alone. Everyone must complete this journey, with courage, pride, and Mindfulness.

Pain is an inevitable part of life. Pain can take any form of physical hardships, emotional grief, worry or disappointment. Pain is both a physical sensation and emotional distress, and is often, amplified by emotional distress or trauma. As our body resists pain, it adds another layer of experience.

In this view, pain and resistance are two different layers of the same inner experience.

The core idea is that Pain is unavoidable, but Suffering however can be turned into optional. Suffering arises from our reaction to the pain. This reaction can be a Resistance to that pain or Denial.

Pain is the first layer. It is natural and unavoidable. It's the body and mind responding to what has happened.

Pain carries information, it signals that something needs attention in the body.

Resistance: the second layer, it is the mind tightening around the discomfort, replaying it, fighting it, or trying to suppress it. Resistance arises when the struggle to deny the discomfort begins, or when we try to suppress our thoughts or feelings. Suppression itself is denial.

Suffering, however, begins when we start resisting that pain. When we try to suppress our thoughts and feelings, they often become stronger and rebound back more intensely. Suppressing is also a form of denial.

Denial prevents us from recognizing our thoughts and exerts resistance in processing our feelings.

Resistance and denial both elevate our suffering.

We might not have control over our circumstances, but mindfulness provides the capability to change our perspective.

Mindfulness may not remove the pain from life, but it transforms the way we look at pain, it helps reduce suffering, merely by bringing a change to our outlook toward our pain.

Instead of saying 'Why is this happening to me?', we begin to see 'This is what happening to me'.

This simple recognition shifts our attitude from resistance to acceptance, from denial to recognition.

Theequation **SUFFERING=PAIN x RESISTANCE** (Kristin Neff, The Mindful Self-Compassion Workbook: A proven way to accept yourself, build inner strength and thrive, 2018)**, attributed to Zen Master**

Shinzen Yong, is a widely admitted concept in Mindfulness and other Philosophies.

The relationship between pain, resistance, and

suffering becomes especially clear when we look at the simple yet profound example of a surgical procedure.

1. During surgical treatment, a patient may be undergoing significant surgical procedures, yet the patient experiences no pain while under anesthesia, because the person is not in a state to exert any resistance. Resistance is zero. Pain in that moment is absolutely zero, because of absence of any Resistance. The nervous system is not fighting to resist what is occurring during procedure.
2. In contrast this with the moments before surgery. Pre-surgical anticipation often intensifies the suffering long before any incision is made. The mind begins to imagine the outcomes of the procedures; this is further elevated while signing a Disclaimer Form way before the surgery starts.

The existing physical pain may aggravate, induces fear and anxiety. As we try to deny our fears, the mind tightens its grip and tries to resist the situation, and as result the suffering intensifies.

3. When the person is back from anesthesia, pain may return, and the suffering varies.

A person who understands, accepts, and allows the sensations to be present often suffers less than one who tenses, resists, or mentally argues with what is already happening.

Suffering is proportionate to the Resistance we offer.

We may modify and formulate the
Suffering α Resistance x **Pain**.

This representation reveals that pain is not always within our control, but resistance often is. Suffering emerges not merely from what we feel, but from how strongly we oppose the reality of that feeling.

How to soften resistance and meet life with CALM.

Resistance is anything that goes against your will. "Why this happened to me"; "I do not want this way"

Mindfulness and self-compassion help to reduce the Suffering by lessening the mental Resistance to a situation. CALM is an excellent technique, that may help in reducing our suffering.

C	Consciously, connect to the present moment and bring your attention to physical sensations. Recognize the pain and emotions. without trying to change anything.	Rate the pain from 1-10 and label the emotions. When you notice 'Resistance', label it "This is a moment of resistance" This anchors you in the present moment and interrupts mental resistance.
A	Allow-Acknowledge-Accept the pain and emotions. Let the experience flow as it is. Instead of resisting the pain or denying it, silently say: "This is what's here right now." "This is a moment of suffering" Allowing does not mean liking the pain; it means stopping the struggle against it.	When we allow the situation to exist, and simply accept it as it is, we are purposely reducing the Resistance and letting go the inner struggle.

L	Listen to your inner experience with curiosity and compassion.	Pain carries information. Listening with kindness helps the nervous system feel safe enough to soften. Notice if you are feeling tightness, tension on any part of body, check for any clenching in jaws. Loosen the grip and relax the parts that are most stressed.
M	Meet yourself with compassion. Mindfully Nurture yourself with kindness and understanding and mindfully move on to the next moment.	When we allow the situation to exist, and simply accept it as it is, we are purposely reducing the Resistance and letting go the inner struggle.

Resource:

Mindfulness Session 9:
Mindfulness Practice- Acceptance and Resistance

"Welcome to another session of mindfulness practice."

In this session, we will explore the essence of mindfulness.

As we have discussed in our previous sessions, mindfulness encourages us to be fully aware of the present moment, embracing it moment by moment with acceptance and a non-judgmental, non-resistant attitude.

Resistance, in this context, refers to the inner struggle that arises when we believe our present experience should be different from what it is.

"Now, let's explore the concept of resistance through a common daily experience."

Consider those moments when you've found yourself stuck in traffic during peak rush hours, either running late for work or eager to get home.

It's natural to begin feeling anxious and frustrated.

"These feelings of frustration and anxiety stem from resistance, specifically "resistance toward the current situation."

This is resistance in thoughts and actions.

On the other hand, when we accept that traffic during rush hour is something to be expected, we realize that getting upset won't make the traffic move any faster.

Instead, we might choose to play some calming music and make plans to avoid such situations in the future.

Even though you don't like the situation, you

acknowledge it and respond with a more constructive mindset.

This is acceptance in thoughts and actions.

"Another common form of resistance in psychology is denial."

It refers to a defense mechanism that individuals employ to cope with unpleasant or distressing thoughts, emotions, or realities by refusing to acknowledge their existence or significance.

While denial can serve as a short-term protective mechanism, allowing individuals to shield themselves from dealing with difficult emotions or situations.

It often results in increased suffering in the long run.

This is because avoiding problems or emotions doesn't resolve them; instead, they may accumulate, causing greater suffering in the future.

In summary, while denial can provide temporary relief, it is not a healthy long-term coping strategy.

"Research shows that when individuals attempt to suppress their unwanted thoughts or emotions, those thoughts and emotions often intensify."

"The act of avoiding or suppressing thoughts and emotions impairs one's ability to perceive and respond to emotions and thoughts effectively."

"In conclusion, resistance to unfavorable situations often results in heightened suffering, manifested through intense emotional reactions, denial, or avoidance."

"Mindfulness and acceptance practices play a crucial role in mitigating suffering caused by resistance.

Mindfulness ultimately contributes to the alleviation of distress and the cultivation of a profound inner peace and resilience."

Suffering results from the combination of actual pain or discomfort along with the mental resistance or struggle that we apply to the situation.

"While pain is inevitable, recognizing that we are applying mental resistance can help reduce our suffering."

In the upcoming session, we will continue our exploration to gain a deeper understanding of pain and suffering.

Thank you for joining us, and we look forward to having you in the next session.

See you all in our next session, take care and stay tuned.

(Kristin Neff, The Mindful Self-Compassion Workbook: A proven way to accept yourself, build inner strength and thrive, 2018)

CHAPTER 10
Heal-Thy:
A Mindful Roadmap to Healthy Relations

Healthy relationships are not built on perfection, or getting everything done the right way, rather, they are built on the foundations of understanding and mutual respect. When relationships are supported with respect and awareness, they deepen our sense of connectivity and coherence.

The word 'Healthy' can be gently understood as **"Heal-thy",** meaning, relationships thrive when each person works to heal themselves first.

It reminds that health, especially in relationships-begins within.

The healing of your inner self, nurtured with love and empathy.

Relationships flourish when each person works to heal themselves first.

When each person in relationship practices **"heal-thy"** caring for their own awareness, actions, and words-the relationship becomes **healthy**, grounded, respectful, and resilient.

Heal-Thy heart, Heal-Thy mind.
When both hearts practice Heal-Thy,
The relationship becomes Healthy

There is an ancient Japanese art of fixing the broken ceramic or glass items, called Kintsugi, which means "golden joinery." This technique uses powdered gold or silver mixed with lacquer as a binding material, making perfect bond. It highlights the cracks instead of hiding them.

Kintsugi embrace the imperfections. Accepting the imperfection of life and turning the more beautiful and valuable.

Relationships are delicate and fragile and need to be carried with utmost care and trust. They get strengthened with a feeling of ease and security, much like Kintsugi, where we try to repair the broken, strengthening the bond and turning the weakness into strength in a more meaningful way.

It is said that Relationships and marriages may be made in heaven, in the blue skies, but let's not take it for granted, the relationships require a regular maintenance and, to preserve those relationships, one essentially need to nurture the relationships with love and care, right here the blue skies, on this blue planet, our Earth. Upholding a continual harmonious relationship takes effort- an ongoing effort of subtle care and gentle thoughtfulness. It's a continuous process- a series of small, mindful gestures that keep trust alive.

For sometimes, it feels like an effortless walk, and other time that may seem like a tightrope.

Every relationship at times goes through difficult patches of life but remember the ancient art of Kintsugi.

When we start noticing the invisible moments when your partner cared, quietly, offering comfort and support without seeking acknowledgment. These are the moments that truly sustain the relationships together.

Here is a hypothetical but very common discussion between a married couple on any working day

(Scenario 1)

"Thank goodness, you are not late today, did you pick my medication from pharmacy right next to your workplace?"

"Okay, I totally forgot, I was so involved in my team meeting today, but you could have reminded me."

"Haha, you proved me right again, you didn't pick the stuff as I was expecting, I just wish you proved yourself more useful and reliable."

"What do you mean? I am always here for you, I am the one who brings all the groceries, washes dishes. You even don't know how to get your car for service? I don't want to be harsh, but I need to have more respect."

It is often the smallest moments that define the health of a relationship. While these interactions seem small, they reveal the true emotional pulse between two people. We are constantly managing these tiny exchanges, where a single word can either strengthen our connection or act as another strain that chips away at it.

This communication could have ended in a totally different tone.

(Scenario 2)

"Thank goodness you're not late today. Were you able to pick up my medication from the pharmacy near your workplace?"

"Oh! I'm sorry- I completely forgot. I was so involved in my team meeting today and it slipped my mind; I will get the medicine right now."

"Okay, thank you for telling me honestly. I know work gets intense sometimes. The medication is important to me, but a massage would really help me right now"

"Sure, I have magic in my hands, will massage like a pro, and I appreciate your understanding, I have set a reminder to pick up medication, first thing tomorrow morning, we're a team."

"Thanks, I rely on you a lot, and maybe I don't say

that enough. What matters most to me is that we respect each other and communicate when something slips."

While the interactions seem small, they reveal the true emotional pulse between two people. We are constantly managing these small exchanges, where a single word can either strengthen our connection or may create a crack.

Agitated relationships often arise when both people are trying to validate themselves at the same time. When each person is focused on being seen, heard, and justified, there's little space left to truly listen. What begins as a simple issue quickly becomes a struggle for recognition.

We start seeking validation from our partner.

Four pillars of "Heal-thy"

Pillar # 1
Heal Yourself Before Reacting (Heal-Thyself)

Notice your emotions before speaking. Take a brief pause instead of reacting.

Respond mindfully. Slowing down during emotional moments preserves dignity on both sides.

Mindfulness invites us to move toward each other, even in small ways.

Listening without distraction, responding when our partner reaches out, and staying emotionally present all signal care. These choices build trust and a feeling of collaboration.

Being mindful helps in moments of conflict.

We focus on the issue rather than attacking our partner. We speak gently, take responsibility for our part, and avoid harsh words that cause lasting harm.

Mindfulness also teaches openness.

We allow our partner's perspective to matter, even when we disagree. Letting another person influence us is not weakness- it is respect in action.

Some differences cannot be fixed, and mindfulness helps us accept this.

When we stop trying to change or defeat our partner, tension softens. Respect grows when differences are allowed to exist without judgment.

Finally, mindfulness helps couples build meaning together.

Shared routines, values, and intentions give the relationship direction. They remind both partners why they choose to stay connected, even during difficult times.

In a continued relationship, respect, if maintained by force or fear cannot last long.

Respect can only be sustained through awareness, kindness, and restraint.

When we stay mindful, we protect our own dignity and other's too.

And where dignity is protected, respect naturally continues to grow.

Pillar # 2
Protect Dignity of each other (Heal-Thy Space)

Healthy relationships ask us to remain aware and compassionate.

To heal the relationship, we begin by slowing down.

We notice our reactions before they become words. We choose to care over being right. This pause alone can soften years of tension.

To heal the connection, we protect dignity.

We speak without cruelty. We listen without preparing our defense. Even in disagreement, we remember that the other person is not the enemy.

To heal the bond, we take responsibility without self-attack or accusation.

We acknowledge our part, not to carry guilt, but to restore balance. Accountability builds trust where excuses cannot.

To heal the shared space, we accept differences instead of trying to fix or change each other.

Some differences are not problems to solve but realities to respect. Acceptance brings peace where control only creates resistance.

Mindfulness keeps the relationship alive and successful.

And where mindfulness lives, respect continues to grow.

To heal the space between two people, we honor what is good, even when things are hard.

When your actions stay aligned with your values, even during conflict, you are creating a safety buffer.

People may forget arguments or leave relationships, but they remember how safe or unsafe they felt with someone. That feeling becomes the emotional safety buffer they carry within the relationship.

Pillar # 3
Honor-Thy Differences

Accept that two individuals can differ in their opinions, feelings and responds. Acknowledge differences provide opportunity to learn, grow and understand each other. Understand and honor the differences. Acknowledge that some disagreements are about values, not right or wrong. Respect differences without trying to control or fix the other person. In a continued relationship, respect is not a single activity, it is a daily practice.

It grows when we slow down, listen deeply, and respond with kindness.

It survives when we choose understanding over judgment and care over control.

- Understand that some disagreements are about values, not right or wrong.
- Respect differences without trying to control or fix the other person.

Pillar # 4
Appreciate Small Moments (Cherish-Thy Moments)

Notice and appreciate the small moments of everyday life.

These small moments and simple and an honest gesture of appreciation build the strength of a lasting relationship.

Healing does not require grand gestures. It grows through small moments of awareness, kindness, and shared laughter.

- Notice the little acts of care your partner or friend shows.
- Celebrate the efforts, and not just outcomes.

Appreciating small moments and acknowledge one small thing the other person did that matter.

Together, these Four pillars of "Heal-thy" guide a relationship towards awareness, harmony, acceptance and wellbeing.

Here is a dialogue from popular sitcom (The Modern Family) which aired in 2010. Featuring a character Phil during his visit to a Spa. Phil starts random chat with ladies around in the Spa and got some good advice.

Ladies advise: *"When your partner tells you that she* *has a problem, do not jump in with solutions until she asks for help.?"*

Phil: *okay, I am confused, you are saying if she tells me she has a problem I am not supposed to help her.*

Lady at Saloon*: Not at all, unless she asks for your help...*

Phil: *but if she let me know, I can let her problem go away.*

Ladies advise: *'When you say do this or do that, all she is hearing is that I am smarter than you.*

Ladies advise*: she doesn't want you to solve her problems, she just wants your support so that she can solve her problems herself, and...*

Other Lady at Saloon: *sometimes she just wants a sympathetic ear.*

Phil: *woo wow, that just makes a sense, ladies, so if Claire says I hate getting stuck in traffic.*

Phil: *I shouldn't say, "maybe you should leave earlier or don't get on the freeway."*

Phil: *I should just say, "I know that's so frustrating."*

Everyone cheers!!...

The scene from Modern Family is a classic example of bridging the gap between solving or fixing a problem verses providing emotional support and validating.

The CALM technique is a communication skill under mindfulness framework. It is a way of remembering how to stay connected and choose response over reacting. Instead of seeking validation first, it invites us to offer presence first.

The CALM technique offers a simple, grounded way to disconnect your struggle for seeking validation and connect to Listening to and validating your partner, while finding a solution becomes secondary.

Often, partners feel a strong urge to offer answers. Yet in those moments, what they really seek is to be heard. They may be looking for emotional validation and support- and deep down, they already know that you are there for them when it truly matters.

CALM is not meant to suppress conflict. It helps transform conflict into understanding and growth.

Instead of reacting from emotion, we respond with awareness, instead of attacking each other, we work together to understand the deeper need. In this way, conflict becomes an opportunity for clarity and building trust.

CALM technique re-orders the problem and the solution to that problem. It places listening and validating the problem first, while finding the solution becomes secondary, or even getting the solution to the problem was never intended.

CALM Practice in moments of conflict	Mental steps during CALM Practice	Outcome of CALM Practice
C- Connect and Compose Yourself (Check-In)	Pause and focus on the person before responding. Show that you care about their feelings. Connection comes before solutions. Before you speak, locate the conflict within your body. Notice for any tightening, the heat, the contraction. Instead of looking at what the other person is doing "wrong," look at what is happening inside you. Conflict begins as sensation before it becomes story. Ask softly: What is happening inside me right now? Where do I feel this in my body?	You move from autopilot to awareness. Instead of reacting instantly, you become a witness to your own emotions.
A- Acknowledge the Emotions	Notice both your own feelings and theirs. Speak about emotions gently and without blame. Offer validation to the concern without conditions.	Your attitude shifts from judgment to understanding. Emotional tension softens and openness begins.

L- Listen, understand and locate the Core	Listen to understand, not to respond. Venting releases pressure. Once emotions settle, clarity returns on its own. Sometimes being fully heard is the most important solution. Try to listen, understand and locate the Core; listen to the underlying meaning, not just words.	The conversation moves from reactive to responsive. Clarity begins to replace confusion.
M- Move Toward Mutual Understanding- Manifest with Presence and speak mindfully	After listening, explore solutions as a team. Focus on collaboration rather than blame or control. Agree on practical steps that respect both people. Respond with respect, replace advice with validation and appreciation. Instead of blaming, you offer information. "I felt disconnected when we didn't talk today. I realize I need a little more shared time."	You return to the relationship as partners rather than opponents. The dynamic shifts from adversary to ally.

CALM Practice within the Heal-Thy Approach

CALM is the practice; Heal-Thy is the foundation.

Heal-Thy reminds us that every relationship begins with awareness within ourselves. CALM becomes the practical way to apply this understanding during moments of conflict. It guides us to pause, reflect, and respond with care rather than react with impulse.

CALM Practice	Heal-Thy Focus	Inner Shift
Connect and Compose Yourself-Check-In-Scan	When you connect with yourself first, you create space for understanding instead of escalation.	This moment of awareness helps you step out of automatic reaction-a shift from Autopilot to attentive Engagement.
Acknowledge the Emotions	Acknowledging emotions brings compassion into the conversation.	Validation allows emotions to settle and opens the door to honest conversation-a shift from Resistance to Acceptance.
Listen, understand and locate the Core of the experience	Acknowledging emotions brings compassion into the conversation.	Often, the real issue lies beneath the noise on the surface. Looking beyond the surface noise and recognize deeper concern-a shift from surface noise to inner clarity.
Manifest with Presence	Responsibility and Respect makes Relationships stronger, When both persons work together rather than against each other.	Relationships grow stronger when both people work together rather than against each other-a shift Adversary to Collaborator.

When one person chooses CALM, agitation softens- and connection becomes possible again.

Phil learned that instead of rushing to offer a solution, one needs to remain calm and hear what one's partner is feeling. Good practice in a relationship is to put all distractions away, make eye contact while listening. Respond with respect, replace advice with validation and appreciation.

We may try using words like

- "I see your point."
- "I understand your perspective"
- "That makes sense."
- "That must have been stressful."
- "We are a team, on the same side."

In Heal-Thy, conflict is not something to eliminate or fear. It is something to reclaim.

A reclaimed conflict is a moment of tension that has been brought back into relationship- with awareness, self-compassion, and responsibility. It is conflict that no longer seeks to win or wound, but to reveal. When reclaimed, disagreement becomes information rather than accusation.

Heal-Thy invites us to befriend the feud by first turning inward. Before reaching for repair with another, we attend to our own nervous system, our own unmet needs, our own tenderness. This inner repair is what prevents conflict from becoming contaminated.

In reclaimed conflict:

- We pause instead of reacting.
- We validate without abandoning ourselves.
- We speak from presence, not protection.

Here, conflict becomes a bridge rather than a rupture. It shows us where care is needed, where boundaries are forming, and where growth is asking to occur.

Reclaimed conflict restores equality. Two people meet again- not as adversaries, but as collaborators in understanding. The relationship returns to friendship not because the conflict disappeared, but because it was held with warmth.

By truly listening to partner's perspective, tension becomes understanding and understanding restores connection.

Just like a skilled tennis player checks the tension of his racket strings while focusing on the ball. The tension in the strings is not a background detail, but it shapes the entire game. The right amount of tension makes all the difference.

The same is for a guitar player. Only a fine-tuned guitar can make a produce beautiful music.

Relationships move by the same principle. Connection flourishes when the tension is not ignored or suppressed but gently adjusted with awareness and wisdom.

When we listen to each other carefully, a fine-tuned emotional space is created, building a harmony and peace.

Some tension is natural. In fact, it is necessary. It allows feelings to surface instead of being suppressed. It creates room to express discomfort, to clarify misunderstandings, to adjust and grow. Without tension, a relationship becomes vague and unstructured- pleasant perhaps, but lacking direction.

A relationship that can tolerate tension becomes resilient. It can absorb impact. It can stretch without breaking and it remains alive.

The goal is not to eliminate tension. It is to learn how to hold it wisely.

"Please note that The CALM technique is offered as a general framework for mindful communication in everyday relationships. It is not intended to replace marriage counseling or professional support. You're welcome to test this out in your daily routine and discover what feels right for you."

SECTION III

CHAPTER 11
BREATH- A Bridge to the Universe

It is indeed the greatest paradox of our life; the one thing that keeps us alive is the thing we notice the least. Breath always stays with us, right from birth until death, yet it goes unnoticed. The whole story of life runs between two points, the story begins with birth, and the story concludes at death, we call it lifespan. Everything changes between these two points except the breath. Only breathing is the constant during the lifespan of an individual.

Child with changes over the years attains adulthood; with passing years the adult person reaches old age. Many seasons come and go, the life changes its colors in various dimensions of life; but breath is always there, always like roots of a tree, holding it strongly against all the odds, always with us.

Breath always here and hence qualifies as a reliable establishing point for remembering the present moment. In the Buddhist context, Sati, a word from Pali language is used to describe mindfulness, which literally means 'To Remember'. In a deeper meaning, Sati is the ability to be attentive and aware of the present moment. With awareness, without getting away with distractions in a non-reactive, non-judgmental way. Each breath brings life energy to us, a vital energy for every cell, and every organ in our body to function.

Pana a Pali word, and ***Prana*** a word from Sanskrit language, translates to the "vital life force", the primary energy that animates all existence in the universe. It is manifested as life and energy.

"It is the Prana that is manifesting as the action of

the body, as a nerve currents, as thought force. The sum total of all the forces in the universe, mental or physical, when resolved back to their original state is the Prana. Prana evolved everything that we call energy, everything that we call force." (Vivekanand, 1947)

Breath is the fundamental life energy that forms a bridge between our body, mind and the Universe. It is not merely a mechanical process of pumping air in and out, but is a complex, self-regulating living process that continuously communicates with the nervous system.

Each inhale provides a lifeline to sustain life, and with each exhale we release the waste that no longer serves any purpose, letting go all the tension, restoring our existence, and maintaining a delicate balance between our internal state and the external world. Though our lungs are functioning automatically, yet they can be controlled consciously, turning them into an ultimate tool for Self-awareness and Self-regulation.

Breathe Normally with an element of awareness

This is not exercise, this is lifestyle. Breathe normally at your natural pace. There is no need to manipulate your breath in any way. Keep on breathing with full awareness. During the inhalation, let your attention travel with the air as it flows into your lungs. Feel the air passing through your nostrils, simply observe it. Move your awareness with breath and silently acknowledge, "I am breathing in."

During exhalation cycle, let your attention follow the moving air, from the lungs, passing through the nostrils, and gently dissolve into the space around you. Move your awareness with breath and silently acknowledge, "I am breathing out."

As Buddha said, ***"Be aware of your breath as it is coming in, and as it goes out"***

Being aware of the incoming breath and the outgoing

air from your nostrils, feel it flowing. Even though we cannot see the air but sense the cool air we inhale and the exhaled warm air from the nostrils. Keep your hand in front of your nostrils and feel the warm exhaled breath flowing out.

At the beginning of inhalation cycle, notice the moment the air touches the nostril, feel it, and as the air travels inward, feel the air flowing through the passage. Just breathe normally and simply be aware of your breath as it is coming in, and as it goes out.

As we bring this practice into our daily life, we begin to develop an awareness of the breath, its deeper presence within us. As we continue our practice of mindful breathing, we become aware of a small interval between each breath. This is the turning point between two breaths.

The point when incoming breath cycle ends and the outgoing breath commences. This brief gap is the moment when the gases exchange in the lungs, oxygen is absorbed as the nourishment for life and the carbon dioxide is released out.

Notice the turning point of breath and watch this brief gap when incoming air turns to outgoing air. See **Point A** in the illustration below.

As we have exhaled the air completely out, and just before beginning to next inhalation cycle, notice another brief pause. This is the fusion point, the turning point where Exhalations turns into Inhalation, the point at very beginning of cycle 2.

See **Point B** in the illustration below.

You may place yourself into practice for watching the gap between breaths, the turning points, the fusion points of the breath for a short interval. Go back to your natural pace and breathe normally. Bring back your awareness on breathing with full awareness, just normal breathing with awareness.

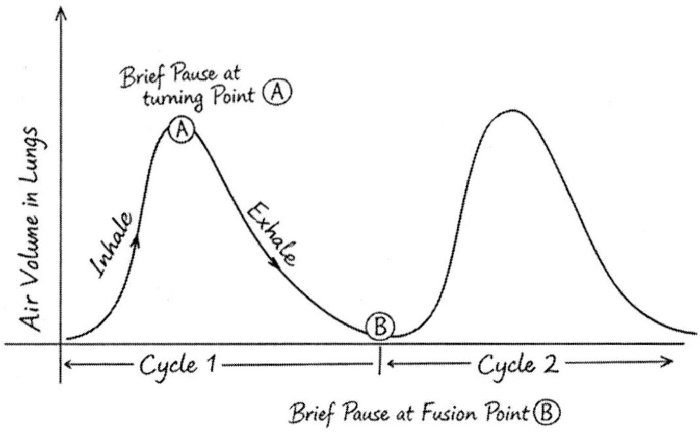

The graph is for ***illustration purposes*** *within the framework of mindfulness.*

Breathing mindfully can help calm our feelings. It recalibrates our emotional state and helps regulate the swings in mood.

There are some other breathing techniques that require **intentional breath controlling** and are helpful in bringing calm and attune to our mood.

1. Square Breathing or Box Breathing (4-4-4-4)

This is a simple and structured breathing technique used to calm our mind and releases stress. We intend to spend an equal amount of time on the inhale, the hold, the exhale, and the release.

Step 1-While we Inhale: Inhale through nose for 4 seconds or for 4 mental counts, think of receiving the **"vital life force",** the Prana and extend your gratefulness.

Step 2- The Hold: Take a gentle pause for 4 seconds or for 4 mental counts. Experience the fullness. Find the silence in those moments, ensure that you are comfortable holding in the breath. (recall point A of the illustration)

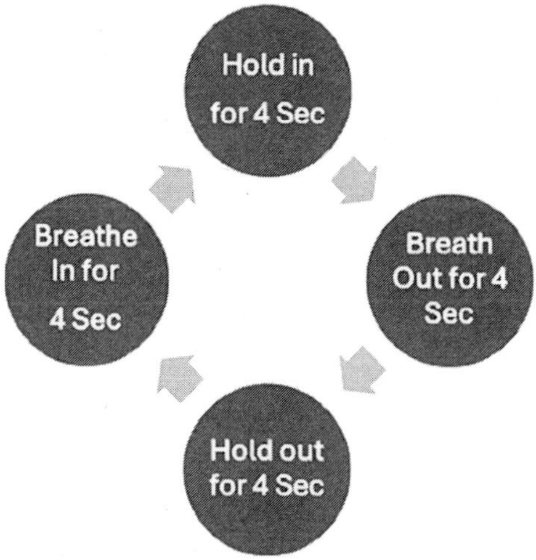

Step 3-The Exhale: Release the air slowly through your nose or mouth. Release the air mixed with unwanted gases and let go all the tension and mental clutter.

Step 4-The Empty Hold: Sit in the stillness. Realize that even when empty, you are okay. (recall point B of the illustration)

Avoid constraining yourself at any point. The purpose of this exercise is to release stress and cultivate calmness. If you try to force or confine yourself strictly into a box, the practice may lose its purpose.

If at any moment the breathing feels overwhelming, gently shift return to your normal breathing, and simply notice with awareness.

2. **Tringle Breathing** -In-Pause-Out (5-4-7)

This is a simple, steady and settling exercise, that helps calm the mind without forcing the breath.

Breath in gently through the nose for 5 seconds

Hold the breath in for 4 seconds

Breath out through the mouth for 7 seconds with a soft "whoosh."

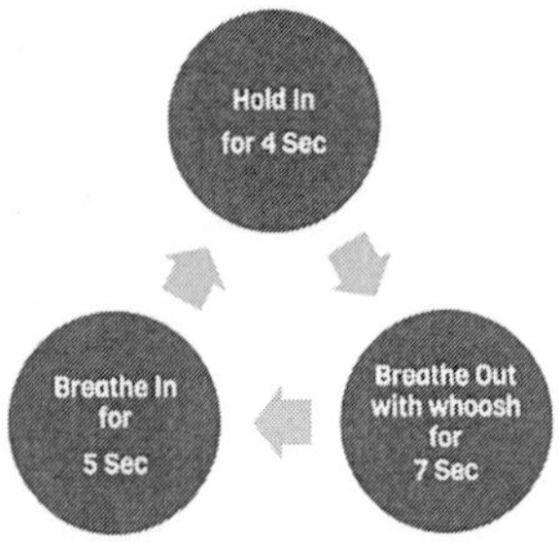

As the air leaves, imagine the tension leaving your shoulders, your jaw, and your mind.

3. Diaphragmatic Breathing

As infants, we are all born breathing through the diaphragm, taking deep, natural breaths. As we grow older, we often develop the habit of breathing through the chest, shifting toward shallower breaths. This change usually happens gradually and unconsciously.

This transition may occur as an adaptation to social and emotional environments. Feelings such as self-consciousness, fear of standing out, or concern about breathing differently can influence our breathing habits. The breath adjusts accordingly to give a feeling of protection.

Diaphragmatic breathing is a gentle mindfulness practice that brings the body back into balance. It helps relax the nervous system and manage stress, especially during moments of pain, tension, or emotional strain.

The practice invites the breath to move deeper into the body, allowing the belly to rise and fall. This form of deep breathing allows the body to exchange more incoming oxygen for outgoing carbon dioxide, supporting more efficient breathing.

As the breath slows, our nervous system begins to settle, heart rate eases, muscles soften and the body shifts out of fight-or-flight and into a state of calm presence.

This practice is not about controlling the breath or forcing relaxation.

It is about listening, allowing, and returning- again and again- to the natural rhythm of the breath.

With regular practice, diaphragmatic breathing can:

- Reduce anxiety
- Increase focus
- Calm emotional reactivity
- Create a felt sense of safety and steadiness

Diaphragmatic breathing can be learned and practiced while sitting, standing, or lying on your back.

Place one hand on your stomach, just above the belly button, and the other hand on your chest. Breathe in slowly through your nose, imagining a balloon filling in your stomach. You will feel the hand on your belly rise as the abdomen expands, while the hand on your chest remains relatively still.

Breathe out slowly through your mouth, imagining the balloon gently shrinking as your stomach softens and flattens.

When slow, diaphragmatic breathing is combined with counting backward, the mind is given a steady, neutral anchor. The counting gently interrupts anxious loops and mental background noise, while the deep breath soothes the body from the inside out.

It is important to remember, try not to hold the inhaled breath inside for long, Recall **Point A**, the turning point where the gas exchange happens.

Lungs have already absorbed Oxygen and released Carbon dioxide, that needs to be released. You do not want to hold unwanted gas trapped inside your lungs.

When we hold our breath, consciously or unconsciously, we aren't just trapping gases, but we are physically holding onto stress, tension, and anxiety. If you are feeling stressed or anxious, go back to your natural breathing, at your normal pace.

Alternate Nostril Breathing (Mindfulness Perspective) (Swami Vivekanand, 1893)

Alternate nostril breathing is a type of yogic breathing that may help reduce anxiety and stress.

It is also a way of training the mind through awareness of the breath.

From perspective of mindfulness, breath is always happening in the present moment and when we pay attention to it, the mind naturally settles.

As we breathe in through one nostril and breathe out through the other, our attention has something simple and steady to rest on. This reduces mental wandering and brings the mind back to now.

Here is a brief **Alternate Nostril** Breathing (ANB) exercise, note that we will use our right thumb to close our right nostril and ring finger to close our left nostril, alternatively as illustrated.

To begin with, sit comfortably and relax your shoulders.

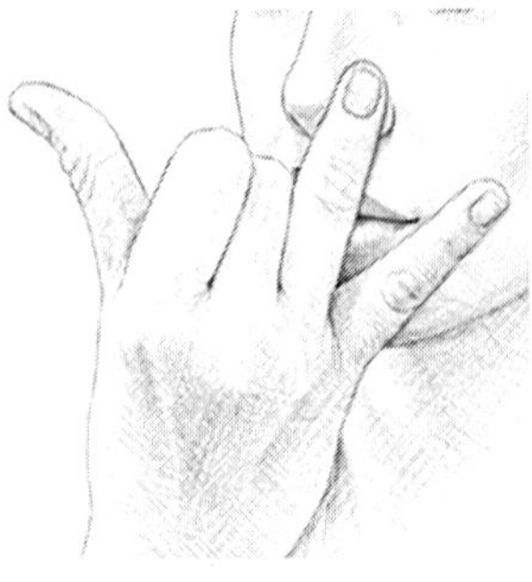

1. Inhale from Right Nostril: Close your Left Nostril and Inhale deeply through the Right Nostril.
2. Switch: Now switch the positions by closing the Right Nostril and Exhale through the Left Nostril.
3. Inhale from Left Nostril: Again, inhale through the Left Nostril, while the right nostril is closed
4. Exhale Right: Finally, Close your left nostril and exhale through the right nostril.
5. This makes a one complete cycle of **Alternate Nostril** Breathing.

Repeat ANB for five times, if you feel comfortable.

Self-reflection:

Notice if the mind is calmer?

Is awareness clearer? Do you feel quieter?

Alternate Nostril Breathing (ANB) exercise				
Steps	**Left Nostril**	**Right Nostril**	**Breath Direction**	**Mindfulness focus**
Step 1: Close Left Nostril and Inhale through the Right Nostril.	Closed	Open	Inhale	Notice the cool air entering, feel the expansion while inhaling.
Step 2: Switch, Close Right Nostril and Exhale through the Left Nostril.	Open	Closed	Exhale	Observe the release, let go all the tension.

Step 3: keep the Right Nostril closed and Inhale through the Left Nostril.	Open	Closed	Inhale	Invite steadiness, and feel a sense of balance and equanimity.
Step 4: Close Left Nostril and Exhale through the Right Nostril.	Closed	Open	Exhale	Experience completion and return to the center.

One full cycle involves breathing in and out of both sides. You always switch nostrils after an inhalation and stay on the same side after an exhalation. This pattern helps balance the nervous systems.

Move slowly and comfortably. Do not force the breath. Notice the calming effect on your body and mind. This simple practice restores balance and gently brings you back to center.

By alternating the breath, the body and mind gradually move toward equilibrium.

There is no need to control the breath or hold it forcefully. Mindfulness means observing, not manipulating. Let the breath be smooth and natural. If there is a pause, let it happen on its own.

As you practice **Alternate Nostril** Breathing (ANB) (Çöme O, 2025), you may begin to notice:

- A calming of emotional reactivity
- A steadier mood
- Greater clarity and focus

This happens because attention is no longer pulled by

thoughts and feelings. It is gently anchored in the physical sensation of breathing.

If the mind wanders, simply notice that it has wandered and return your attention to the next inhalation or exhalation. Each return is part of the practice.

In this way, alternate nostril breathing becomes less about technique and more about presence- a quiet meeting of breath, body, and awareness.

A study aimed to assess the effectiveness of alternate nostril breathing (ANB) as a non-pharmacological intervention to reduce the frequency and severity of migraine attacks and associated disability in adult patients. The conclusions were promising. ANB significantly reduced migraine frequency and disability, making it a promising non-invasive and accessible treatment option for migraine management.

Resource:

.

Mindfulness Session 10:
Mindful Practice on Breath (Kabat-Zinn, 2014)

This is a 3-minute guided meditation program designed to promote deep relaxation and to build a unique restful awareness Set aside a few moments when you are not occupied with any sort of activity, away from all distractions Follow these instructions as they say to do To begin with, Let's sit in a dignified and comfortable posture with eyes closed gently.

Bring your attention to the fact that you are breathing Focus wherever you feel your breath most prominently.

It may be at the tip of your nose, chest, abdomen, or entirely from your nose to abdomen Breathe normally.

Notice the full duration of your breath. There is no need to manipulate your breath in any way.

Now, direct your attention to your belly, your abdomen and feel the sensations.

The rise and fall of the belly,

Breath-by-breath,

Moment-by-moment.

Allow your attention to remain here, for a short while.

Just follow the rhythmic movements of your belly with each breath,

With Awareness.

With Mindfulness.

CHAPTER 12
Letting Go
Finding Freedom in Forgiveness

We all get hurt- often by the very people we trust the most. And when that trust collapses, it leaves behind some invisible wounds, the wounds of emotional memory that keep on simmering inside, quietly.

Over time, as we carry these scars, they begin to shape our perception, the way we see life, it changes our viewpoint towards how we see ourselves and everyone else.

Psychology calls this Schema formation-the mind starts building the beliefs based on our past scars. It starts challenging our core beliefs about safety, self-worth and trust in others.

Maybe there is certain scar you are still holding onto. You may genuinely want to get rid of that pain, but you just have not figured out how to let it go, or the hurts are too deep to simply forgive and move on.

We need to shield our vulnerability before we are in position to forgive someone who has harmed us or has been abusing us in a relationship.

The other aspect of vulnerability is also applicable.

If we are causing harm to someone in a relationship, intentionally or without intending it.

If we are doing harm to our partner in a relationship, it is important to pause and face what is really happening. Facing the harm to what we have done can be helpful.

Forgiveness is not something that can be forced

through our willpower or forced by others. Forgiveness is an emotional process that requires healing and compassion.

Compassion emerges from the heart of mindfulness when we meet our sufferings, and Mindfulness invites us to open to our sufferings with love and awareness.

By merely saying 'I forgive you' may not be genuine forgiveness as a residue of resentment always stays, rooted deep within.

Forgiveness if it didn't matter, by just saying 'it's okay', it is not denial or erasing the pain- it's awareness. It's not a weakness, its inner strength.

There are times when the pain is circumstantial and not caused by anyone. We acknowledge that the suffering arises from the situation itself, something much larger than our personal will or control.

In such moments, there is no one to blame, no grievance to hold. There is only the quiet truth of what life has placed before us.

At times, we have to move across the country to start a new life, leaving our friends and family behind, or when we move across countries, leaving our elderly parents in agony, we carry guilt with us that we fail to pay attention and care for what they need.

And when we recognize this fact, grieving becomes an act of modesty and acceptance- an opening of the heart to what is, rather than holding to what should have been. It is in this soft, honest space that healing slowly begins.

Forgiveness, in this sense, comes through awareness, we learn to hold our pain with compassion rather than resistance. The heart begins to soften, not by force, but by willingness.

Forgiving can unfold through the practice of **CALM,** when we take a pause and connect to the present moment, we begin to sense the undercurrent of pain.

It is a conscious, step-by-step act of releasing your tight grip on resentment and bitter thoughts.

When we address them with CALM, we move from tightness to understanding, from heaviness to clarity, and from reactivity to compassion- toward ourselves and others.

(Connect with Present moment- Acknowledge, Allow and Accept- Listen to your inner experience with curiosity- Mindfully Nurture yourself)

CALM is a four-step way to pull ourselves out of suffering and remorse. It is guiding the mind back to steadiness and compassion.

C- Consciously connect with the present moment.

Open yourself to the pain and distress you are going through and offer yourself gentle care and tenderness.

A- Acknowledge your feelings

You have been hurt and allow your heart to melt with sympathy for the pain. Allow yourself to open to grieve.

Grieving is an important part of healing because it helps us face the truth of what happened and how deeply it affected us. When we skip this step, forgiveness can become shallow or forced.

Grieving means giving ourselves permission to feel sadness, disappointment, or anger that came with the hurt. It's a way of honoring our pain instead of pretending it doesn't matter. Sometimes we cry, reflect, or simply sit with the feeling of loss. Through this process, we begin to understand our own suffering more clearly.

As we grieve, something gentle starts to happen inside us- the tightness around the heart begins to loosen.

The pain softens, and we create space for understanding and compassion. Only then can forgiveness arise naturally, not as an act of will, but as a quiet unfolding of the heart.

It matters because we cannot heal or grow if we ignore the pain we've caused. When we hurt someone, even unintentionally, a part of us knows it- and that awareness can bring feelings of remorse, guilt, or sadness. These emotions are not meant to punish us; they're signals from our conscience, inviting us to look deeper.

By opening to these feelings instead of avoiding them, we take responsibility for our actions. We begin to understand the impact we've had on another person's heart. This honest acknowledgment softens our defenses and helps us reconnect with our own humanity.

If we try to forgive ourselves without facing this inner pain, the forgiveness will feel empty or incomplete. But when we allow ourselves to feel the remorse fully, something changes within us- we grow in empathy, humility, and wisdom. In that tenderness, true self-forgiveness becomes possible.

When someone has harmed us, we feel hurt, and a wave of bitterness often arises. In such moments, the most compassionate thing we can do- for ourselves- is to forgive.

When we skip this step, forgiveness can become shallow or forced.

L- Listen to your inner experiences with curiosity.

As we allow ourselves to open to our feelings and gently say, 'Let it be', we create a space for our thoughts, emotions and feelings arise. Something gentle starts to happen inside us, the tightness around the heart begins to loosen. The pain softens, and we create space for understanding and compassion. Only then can forgiveness arise naturally, not as an act of will, but as a quiet unfolding of the heart.

M- Mindfully Nurture yourself

Mindfulness provides the awareness and non-reactivity needed to see pain clearly.

Nurture yourself with full awareness and intentionally move on to next moment

Forgiveness is not an act of control, but a process of release unfolds naturally when the conditions are right. It arises naturally when we no longer wish to carry the burden of resentment. In that moment, forgiveness becomes what it was always meant to be- not a favor to another, but a return to inner peace.

In essence you cannot make forgiveness happen through willpower, but you can prepare the ground through willingness and in that openness, forgiveness finds you.

Why is the four step CALM for Forgiveness important?

Forgiveness is a switch we can flip. It's a gradual unwinding of emotional tension, not an act of mental command. The idea of Forgiveness includes 'forgiveness to others' and 'forgiveness to yourself'.

You may simply say "I forgive", but, the residual of resentment and anger still reside within you, you did not let go your resentment and agony genuine.

Emotional healing takes its own time and forgiveness unfolds naturally, at its own pace, just waiting for right conditions.

Forgiveness is not an act of control but a process of release, it is allowing rather than imposing.

It is important to open to the hurt we are experiencing, and equally important to open to the pain, remorse and guilt of hurting others.

Practicing CALM develops a shift in attitude, from

forcing to allowing "I may not be able to forgive now, but I am willing to let forgiveness work through me."

This willingness softens the inner resistance that keeps pain alive, making space for compassion and understanding to grow. Willingness is the seed of transformation. You stay present with your pain without judgment, and through awareness, the grip of resentment loosens on its own and the anger soften.

In the Office-

Workplaces, though less intimate, can also be emotionally complex.

Imagine a situation in office:

You discussed the solution for fixing that issue with your colleagues. After days of pressure across the management team, you were able to figure out solution to a problem that no one else could see. You share it with your colleagues, trusting the collaborative spirit of the group. But when the meeting begins, something unexpected happens.

As an element of surprise, during the meeting one of the colleagues, Kelley took the credit for your idea. It is fairly natural to get annoyed. Kelly steps forward and presents your idea as her own.

In that moment, it's natural for irritation to rise. Anger flares because it isn't just a matter of credit; it's the sting of feeling betrayed, the slow erosion of trust.

Even if Kelly apologizes later, the mind continues to replay the event. The hurt doesn't vanish simply because the words "I'm sorry" are spoken.

This is where CALM becomes more than practice, it becomes a lifeline.

Through CALM, the event doesn't disappear- but its grip loosens. The replay softens. You reclaim your sense of presence, clarity, and dignity- not because the situation was resolved perfectly, but because you chose to treat your own heart with care.

Anger may flare up as you feel betrayed and the trust erodes. Even if the person apologizes later, the mind replays the event: "They humiliated me in front of everyone."

Trying to "will" forgiveness might look like forcing yourself to act unaffected- smiling politely while resentment simmers beneath. You're performing forgiveness, not living it.

But being willing transforms the dynamic.

You might say internally: 'I am not ready to forget this yet, but I don't want this resentment to simmer within me'.

This quiet willingness shifts your focus from retaliation to understanding. You begin to see the larger picture- maybe the colleague was acting from insecurity or pressure. The energy of compassion replaces bitterness, not because you willed it, but because you allowed it.

Willingness is the threshold state- the point where the heart starts to unfreeze.

It doesn't demand that you feel differently; it simply asks that you stop resisting the possibility of healing.

In marriage, willingness restores intimacy.

In the workplace, it restores balance.

In both, it reclaims your inner peace- not through force, but through gentle readiness.

Both mindfulness and psychology view forgiveness as a deeply healing process, but not in a moralistic or religious sense. Rather, they see it as a psychological release and a shift in awareness that directly benefits our emotional well-being.

The Tender work of Grieving vs hard shell of Grievance

Grieving	Grievance
Grieving is the tender pain that rises when we lose something or someone we deeply valued- a relationship, a hope, a version of ourselves.	Grievance, on the other hand, is the wound we continue to hold onto when we feel wronged.
Grieving is inward, soft, and human. It is our heart acknowledging, "Something precious is gone."	It is outward, often charged with resentment or a sense of injustice. A grievance says, "Someone hurt me, and I'm still carrying the weight of what they did."
It's a process of feeling, accepting, and slowly integrating the loss into our lives.	It is not about loss alone- it's about the meaning we attach to that hurt, the story we repeat, the bitterness that lingers long after the event has passed.
Grief asks for compassion, patience, and presence. It humbles us and opens us.	Grievance, on the other hand, clings the mind around blame, keeps the wound alive.
Grief softens us.	Grievance hardens us.
Grieving allows speedy healing.	Grievance delays the healing process.
Grieving moves us toward healing. It is soft, honest, and vulnerable. It lets us feel the sadness underneath the hurt so the wound can slowly close.	Grievance keeps us stuck in the hurt. It loops the story of injustice, replaying what happened again and again, tightening the emotional knot instead of loosening it.

CHAPTER 13
Gratitude
A Holistic approach for Well-being

Gratitude is often misunderstood as a polite customary response to pleasant events. We say "thank you" when someone offers help to us. When life goes smoothly our way, the prayers are answered and the outcomes align with our expectations.

But gratitude, in its deepest sense, is far more than a reaction. It is a way of seeing. A way of being.

A holistic approach to well-being invites us to look on the life as a larger picture beyond momentary gains and losses. It asks us to recognize that life is not just a sequence of isolated events but an interconnected flow of experiences, pleasure and pain, fame and anonymity, recognition and denial.

True gratitude does not differentiate between praise and rejection, but it understands that growth can arise from praise as well as from rejection. A word of praise may affirm your path, but a moment of denial may redirect you towards new opportunities.

Gratitude, when practiced consciously, nourishes emotional balance, steadies the restless mind, and opens the heart to trust. It shifts us from scarcity to sufficiency, from entitlement to humility, from control to surrender. In this way, gratitude becomes not just a feeling, but a foundation for well-being.

The Hidden Grace of Existence

Much of life's grace remains invisible. We easily

recognize blessings when they arrive in form of success, health, or harmony. But there is another kind of grace- silent, subtle, and often unnoticed.

Sometimes the deepest blessings are not what happened, but what was averted or what never happened.

There is protection in what we are spared. This hidden grace does not reveal itself. It does not seek recognition yet quietly shapes our journey. Gratitude deepens when we begin to recognize not only the blessings we receive, but also the difficulties we are spared from. As our awareness grows, we begin to see that gratitude itself has layers. It does not always arise in the same depth or maturity. Sometimes it appears as a simple appreciation for favorable outcomes; at other times it evolves into a deeper trust in life itself. In this sense, gratitude exists in different forms or variations. Understanding these layers helps us recognize how our relationship with gratitude can mature over time.

One of the most common and familiar forms is conditional gratitude.

Conditional Gratitude

Conditional gratitude is the most familiar form. It arises when circumstances satisfy our preferences.

"I am grateful because things worked out."

"I am grateful because I received what I wanted."

"I am grateful because life was kind to me."

This form of gratitude is sincere, yet fragile. It depends on outcomes. When events turn unfavorable, gratitude fades and is replaced by complaint, fear, or resentment.

Conditional gratitude keeps us bargaining with life. We are thankful when the universe fulfills our desires, but we withdraw our appreciation when it does not. In this way, gratitude becomes tied to outcomes.

Conditional gratitude appreciates life when it is kind to us, it begins with appreciation for what we receive, while Radical Gratitude goes further beyond conditions. It thanks life for the journey and the way life is unfolding itself.

Radical Gratitude

Radical gratitude rises above outcomes. It means you remain grateful even when things do not go exactly as planned.

If you prepare for a presentation. If it goes well, you are thankful, but if it does not go as expected, you are still thankful- for the experience, the learning, and the courage it took to stand there.

You apply for a position. If you are selected, you will feel grateful, but if you are not selected, you remain grateful, perhaps the role was not meant for you, or perhaps you gained clarity for the next step.

Radical gratitude does not ignore disappointment. It simply does not allow disappointment to erase appreciation.

In practical terms, rising above outcomes means:

- Appreciating effort, not just results.
- Valuing growth, not just recognition.
- Trusting the process, not just the reward.

When gratitude is tied only to success, it is fragile.

When gratitude includes both success and setbacks, it becomes strong.

That strength is called **Radical gratitude.**

In this state gratitude ceases being a "deal", and becomes a way of being...

It is no longer "I am grateful because...", it becomes simply, **"I am grateful."**

This is not passivity or giving up. It is insightful alignment and a humble recognition that the same Universe that gives us life, its grace and free air we breathe in. We accept that its wisdom is bigger than our personal plans and the wisdom is not bound by our expectations.

Radical gratitude moves from the mind to the heart. It softens resistance. It transforms suffering into inquiry. It anchors well-being not in circumstances, but in consciousness.

When gratitude becomes radical, it is no longer an occasional practice- it becomes a way of living.

Gratitude for getting an Opportunity to Serve the needful

When someone gives you a chance to serve, they are offering trust. They are saying, "You are capable."

Feeling grateful for that opportunity is sign of true humility. You recognize that service itself is a privilege. When you feel grateful that you can serve. You realize that you have all that is required, right intention, the skills, time, and ability to make a difference.

You are acknowledging the grace behind your ability. You recognize that your capacity is not entirely self-created. Instead of seeking recognition, you value contribution. Instead of wanting praise, you value participation.

As gratitude deepens, it naturally seeks expression through service. You begin to feel thankful not only for what you have received, but for the opportunity to give. When someone entrusts you with responsibility, when they allow you to help, support, or guide, pause and recognize the grace in that moment.

To serve is not a burden; it is a privilege. Being capable of serving itself a blessing. Gratitude then moves beyond words and becomes participation in the well-being of others.

Gratitude is not only for what we receive. Sometimes, it is for what we are spared.

Recently, a friend and his wife stayed at our home for a Wedding Ceremony.

We were bit worried as his wife has asthma and allergic to cats.

We have a golden retriever dog at home.

There was a quiet concern in the background- What if she has a reaction? What if something triggers and she gets sick?

We even had a backup plan to move them to a hotel just in case.

Thankfully, a week went by, nothing happened. She was perfectly fine and comfortable, and nothing triggered.

The evening remained peaceful, and their stay with us became memorable.

On the surface, it may seem like "nothing had happened."

But that "nothing" was not just an empty word. This “nothing” is absence of trouble, a quite form of Grace.

The Grace that we receive every moment, peacefully. This quite Grace is woven in our daily lives. This is the hidden Grace of our existence.

We often overlook the absence of problems. We notice illness, but not health.

We notice crisis, but not smooth passage.

Gratitude expands when we begin to recognize not only blessings received, but difficulties avoided.

Think of how many times in life could have gone differently?

- A medical report that was normal, the illness that we feared never developed.
- A visit that ended peacefully.
- A conversation that stayed calm.
- The accident that almost happened but averted.
- The conflict was resolved before it could erupt.
- An opportunity that we missed and regretted for, but later realized that was not aligned with our growth.

There are so many outcomes of life that are beyond our control. Universe has all the undisputed power and is free to give and is free to take at its own will.

Our heart continues beating, our lungs continue breathing. We rarely take a pause to notice how much over liver is working hard.

This reflection is meant to build awareness, and not to create fear. Gratitude grows with awareness, with knowing. It recognizes the things could have gone differently.

And when things align gently- when a visit remains harmonious, when a breath flows freely, when the body cooperates- that too is worthy of gratitude.

This is the hidden grace of existence.

"Let one be grateful, humble, and content"*- Traditional Buddha's teaching paraphrased from Dhammapada.*

One of the best ways of cultivating a positive approach towards life is through practice of gratitude. When we start noticing good and hope in our lives, the nourishment and the support that surround us in our day-to-day life, or even in the challenging moments. We start appreciating what we already have in our lives.

By practicing gratitude, we allow ourselves to

recalibrate our perception, reshape our way as we see the world.

Practicing gratitude deepens our sense of being open, grounded and intimately connected to people and the moments that truly matter.

Journaling Gratitude is a great way to achieve mental

Gratitude isn't just about saying thank you; it's the active recognition that we are the beneficiary of a thousand things we haven't created, from the air we breathe to the heart that beats.

and emotional well-being by reducing stress, processing emotions, and improving self-awareness.

Gratitude isn't always spontaneous, but it needs to be nurtured; by giving a gentle invitation to our awareness to see the goodness and kindness we are receiving without noticing it.

Asking yourself certain questions can awaken a sense of appreciation and reconnect you with what's quietly good in your life.

Take a pause and reflect:

- What happened today that was good?
- Even the smallest moment- a smile, a meal, a breath of fresh air- counts.
- What am I taking for granted that I can be thankful for?
- Often, what we overlook the most- health, safety, or simple routines- are what sustain us most deeply.
- Which people in my life am I grateful for?

Think of those who support, understand, or simply walk beside you, even in silence.

- What is the last book I read, or movie, show, or social media clip I truly appreciated and why?

Gratitude can emerge through inspiration and connection, even in small, everyday encounters with art or ideas.

- What am I most looking forward to this week, month, or year- and why?
- Hope itself is a form of gratitude for the possibilities that life still holds.
- What is the kindest thing someone has said or done for me lately?

Let that kindness settle in. Let it remind you that goodness still circulates quietly through human hearts.

Gratitude:
A Conscious Choice for a holistic lifestyle

At its core, Gratitude is a conscious choice. It is an intentional approach toward a holistic way of living. The beauty of honest gratitude is that it cannot be forced. No one can make you feel truly thankful from within.

Gratitude is not about pretending that everything is perfect, but it is about remembering that even in imperfection, there are moments of warmth, care, and meaning.

When you ask these questions sincerely, you don't have to search far for answers- gratitude begins to rise on its own.

Gratitude is a positive emotional state that involves recognizing and appreciating the good things and positive influences in your life. It's not just a feeling, but a practice that can be actively cultivated to increase happiness, improve relationships, and reduce stress.

Gratitude strengthens relationships when they are shared. Expressing appreciation shifts the focus from what you lack to the abundance provided by others.

General Gratitude Expression (Verbal or Written)

"I am thankful for this moment and the peace it brings."

"Gratitude fills me as I recognize all that supports me right now."

"I am grateful for the opportunity to breathe, to pause, and to simply be."

"With each breath, I acknowledge the goodness present in my life."

"I am grateful for the unseen forces that align to support my growth."

'Even in uncertainty, I trust and thank the universe for its quiet wisdom."

"I rest in gratitude, knowing I am supported in countless ways."

(Emmons) *People who cultivate Gratitude in their lives tend to report greater life satisfaction, stronger social bonding and a more meaningful life. Experimental studies confirm that even brief gratitude interventions boost positive effects in life and reduce anxiety and stress. The results of studies demonstrate that acts of gratitude can be used as a therapeutic complement for treating anxiety and depression and can increase positive feelings and emotions in the general population.*

I am intentionally bringing these two themes together- Gratitude and Forgiveness.

At first, they may seem unrelated, while Gratitude celebrates what we have, while forgiveness releases what we hold against ourselves or others.

Both are deeply connected activities of the emotion-

Gratitude and forgiveness are two deeply personal features of human growth. Each carries a quiet power- one releases us from stress, the other uplifts and enriches our being; they act as one letting go, the other letting in.

Forgiveness allows us to let go of the heaviness we've carried for too long, the silent stress that lingers beneath our thoughts. It's not about forgetting what happened but freeing ourselves from the emotional grip of the past.

Forgiveness has many faces.

Sometimes it means releasing the hurt caused by others, choosing not to carry the emotional burden any longer. It's not about approving what happened, but freeing ourselves from the story that keeps replaying in our minds.

At other times, forgiveness turns inward. It asks us to soften toward our own humanity- to meet our mistakes with compassion instead of criticism. Self-forgiveness allows healing to begin where blame once lived. And there are moments, too, when awareness brings the courage to seek forgiveness from those we've hurt. In doing so, we humble the ego and restore the flow of connection.

Gratitude, on the other hand, draws our attention toward what is good and life-giving in the present. It softens our perception, helping us see blessings where we once saw burdens.

Together, they create inner harmony: forgiveness clears the space within, and gratitude fills it with light.

Gratitude is the art of recognizing life's quiet blessings. It invites us to pause and see the goodness already surrounding us, the kindness of others, the lessons wrapped in hardship, the simple breath that sustains us. Gratitude enhances us. It shifts the focus from what's lacking to what's already present, nurturing contentment where restlessness once stood.

Together, forgiveness and gratitude form a cycle of renewal. Forgiveness clears the emotional space within us; gratitude fills that space with light. One releases the heaviness of the past, and the other deepens our appreciation for the present. Without forgiveness, gratitude struggles to take root. Without gratitude, forgiveness feels incomplete.

Mindfulness Meditation Gratitude using CALM

C- Centering Awareness

Before gratitude can deepen, we need to anchor our awareness to the present moment.

Consciously connect with the present moment with full Attention. Centered awareness interrupts the chaos in mind and creates a space for reflection. In this space, gratitude can arise naturally. Radical gratitude begins with presence.

A- Acknowledge and Accept the Grace we are already receiving.

Gratitude begins by recognizing what we already have. Acknowledge the small things you feel grateful for, the unseen blessings, the overlooked grace.

Acceptance is the doorway through which gratitude develops. Allow yourself to feel grateful and gently whisper.

"I am thankful for this breath, for this life moving through me."

"Thank you, universe, for your quiet guidance and constant presence."

"I am grateful for those who have offered kindness, love, and understanding along my way."

L- Listen to your inner experience and Let Go.

Gently recall three good things in your life that you are thankful for. They do not have to be extraordinary, perhaps a staff member in a large store patiently helped you find a product you were looking for, or a door held open or a warm smile from a coffee store cashier.

Gratitude is not about ignoring difficulties but is

about seeing the silver lining amidst challenging times. Listen to inner experience and ask yourself:

"I am grateful to sail through difficult times with strength and resilience."

"Where did I get all this strength from?"

"Who supported me during those difficult times?"

Letting Go transforms our inner resistance into gratitude.

M- Mindfully nurture yourself and a create a Moment of Connection

Inward Gratitude seeks an outward expression of, a meaningful response. Let your outward actions reflect your inward gratitude. Create a moment of connection with yourself.

Notice the qualities that are growing within yourself. Make a moment of connection with others by expressing appreciation, openly and truly.

As you rest in awareness, sense the gentle warmth of gratitude expanding in your heart.

"I am grateful for this moment, this peace, and the gift of simply being. May gratitude guides my thoughts, my words, and my actions."

CHAPTER 14
Escape to connect with Nature

There are times when we feel an urge to step away from all the urgencies and to escape to find a few quite moments.

A few moments of being with yourself as a solitary being are important to rejuvenate, regenerate, and to prevent the burnout. This allows the noise of the world to fade, and take a back seat; so we can listen to our own inner rhythm.

To get those few moments of solitude, you have to discover your own quiet zone. A quiet zone can be anywhere, whether it is morning walk, a corner in a Library or even while commuting.

You must find a quiet zone amidst all noises, as there is no absolute quiet place.

No place is a perfect quiet zone, but, we can still find a moderately quiet corner, where we may enjoy a few solitary mindful moments just with ourselves.

There is no space on earth with as prefect silence.

If you are sitting in a Library, you will still hear someone whispering, or rustling sound of turning the pages.

As you start looking for quietness, you will notice every small sound, humming sound of air Conditioner, the ticking sound of clock, even a slight scratching sound created by pen while someone is writing nearby, every little sound feels like a distraction to you.

We do not always need perfect silence for our

practice, instead we can use the sound as an **object of our focus**. We just need a place where our mind can slow down and breathe.

A place where we can sit in solitary awareness, even if for a few moments.

Sometimes the best way to find peace is simple: **Breathe**; take a few deep and mindful breaths. Feel the warmth of air passing through your nostrils.

Breathe normally and start walking; just to walk around, wander aimlessly, but with full awareness and wit.

Wander without purpose, but with full awareness and curiosity, and let your senses guide you.

Trails, woods, parks, beaches, any space where you feel your breath deepening and your body softens is a good place.

The moment you feel yourself calming down, you've found your zone.

Sometimes, I too, feel an urge to escape from the hurries of urban life, a life that seems like always pushing me to beat the clock.

Quite often, I just step out of my apartment, with no plans in mind. I simply walk out, with no set destination, just walking through, the endless rush, the constant noise of engines, crossing the tall buildings.

On a fine evening, as I stepped farther away from the familiar noise, something subtle shifted.

The city noises suddenly became quieter, and I felt as if I stopped absorbing those noises, and I could hear new sounds-the chirping of birds, a gentle breeze, which most of us has forgotten.

By the time I reached the edge of a trail, I could feel

my breath deeper, as if the trees themselves were inviting me to slow down. The smell in air suddenly changes, earth had a different scent here, intense and initiating.

With each step, I could feel a softened something inside me that the city had hardened.

I do not walk with a destination in mind, but I just walk with awareness and wit.

In nature, I feel free, feel like no one is judging me, nothing judges my pace, nothing measures my worth, everything simply existed and welcomes me as I am.

ART OF DOING NOTHING

It is, strangely, the most difficult task.

We're so used to filling every moment, every silence, and every pause.

When you allow yourself to simply be yourself, something remarkable happens, there is a subtle shift in your attention that transforms your attitude towards things and how you look at them. This brings a new perspective towards our surroundings, with more love and care. Take a look at the trunk of a tree, you will find cracks and flakes peeling away, take a closer look on these shedding flakes-the bark, they have their own stories. Their texture, the moisture, growing moss on their surface, all signal towards a healthy ecosystem.

On more reflective level, a bark tells you that falling is not a failure, rather, nature is creating its own supporting system, and that fallen bark provides shelter to so many living creatures. Nature speaks of acceptance, adaptation and renewal.

Whether you are standing, sitting, or walking, without trying to accomplish anything- you begin to notice, you become aware of the small details you usually overlook.

Noticing the temperature of the air.

The sound of your steps.

The gentle rhythm of your breath.

The quiet thoughts that rise and fall.

In that shift, you discover a quieter world, not around you, but within you.

Trails, woods or parks, any place where you find yourself getting calmer is a great place. In those moments you

Walking on the beach offers a rare balance between motion and stillness. Each wave washes over the sand and withdraws, leaving a clean slate for the next cycle. This natural rhythm mirrors the mind: letting go of what no longer serves and creating space for new thoughts, insights, and creativity to emerge with ease.

In mindfulness practice, this 'Art of doing nothing' could describe a rare but profound moment when the mind becomes completely quiet. The practitioner is simply aware- not doing, not reacting, and not labeling: **Just being.**

You are not in a state of trance, not your feelings, not even your meditative state. You are the one aware of all of it. And in that awareness, you find peace so vast, it feels like resting in the infinite.

This is the most difficult task, but once you master it, it has its infinite potential within.

Notice the shift of your attention.

Here is a refined, coherent version in your style-gentle, reflective, mindful, and human.

It is strangely, the most difficult task. We're so used to filling every moment, every silence, and every pause with wandering thoughts.

But, when you allow yourself to simply be- to stand, sit, or walk without trying to accomplish anything- you begin to notice something remarkable, a shift in your attention is remarkably perceptible.

You become aware of the small details you usually overlook like the temperature of the air, the rhythm of your steps.

The gentle humming sound of your breath. The quiet thoughts that rise and fall without demanding anything from you. This heightened awareness brings a shift within you begin to discover a quieter world within you. The outer world around is just the same.

Resource:

Mindfulness Session 11: Mindfulness & Nature

Welcome back to another session of mindfulness practice. Today, we will be exploring nature and its value in our lives.

Nature serves as a valuable instructor in the art of mindfulness. It teaches us how to be mindful and is a perfect example of "just being."

When you hear sound of birds somewhere in the background or the soft breeze of air touching your face all this gives a connection with the nature, that brings you in "just being" mode, a feeling of resting in present moment and relaxing.

The beauty of connecting with nature lies in its accessibility, whether it's a potted plant adorning your office desk or the allure of a forest trail, nature manifests itself in diverse forms.

From the warmth of a sunlit morning to the enchantment of a starlit night, the melodies of early bird songs to the chorus of crickets in the late hours, Nature gives a sense of relaxation and warmth.

Connecting with nature is like an endless stretch of shining sky, offering both warmth and nourishment to our lives.

Nature is a perfect place to practice mindfulness. You can sit outside, go for a walk, or do a moving meditation. Being outside helps you forget daily stress and focus on what's happening right now.

If possible, let us practice our session outdoors. Find

somewhere outdoors where you won't be disturbed. Close your eyes gently and take a series of deep breaths.

Allow your awareness to embrace the sounds surrounding you. Listen to the most prominent sounds, both near and distant, acknowledging their transient nature. Observe how some sounds rise and slowdown, while others remain constant. Tune into variations in volume and proximity.

Notice how some sounds come and go, while others are constant. Notice how some get louder and softer.

Direct your attention towards the symphony of loud and soft sounds, those that are close and those that are distant. Should your mind wander, gently guide it back to the act of listening.

Open your eyes slowly while maintaining the connection with nature. Observe your surroundings and sense the rejuvenating fresh air around you.

"Nature warmly guides us to embrace the present moment and enjoy it completely."

It offers an opportunities to practice mindfulness through activities like quiet reflection, relaxed walks, or moving meditation.

These activities enable a deeper connection with the surroundings, cultivating a sense of inner peace and self-awareness.

"Despite our hectic daily schedules, try to set aside at least five minutes to spend time outdoors."

See you all in the next session, take care and stay tuned.

SELF - REFLECTION JOURNAL